HOW TO WIN FRIENDS
AND MANAGE REMOTELY

HOW TO WIN
FRIENDS
AND MANAGE
REMOTELY

McKENNA SWEAZEY

CAREER PRESS

This edition first published in 2022 by Career Press, an imprint of
Red Wheel/Weiser, LLC

With offices at:
65 Parker Street, Suite 7
Newburyport, MA 01950
www.careerpress.com
www.redwheelweiser.com

ISBN: 978-1-63265-202-7

Library of Congress Cataloging-in-Publication Data available upon request.

Cover design by Howard Grossman
Interior by Happenstance Type-O-Rama
Typeset in Nobel and Warnock Pro

Printed in the United States of America
IBI

10 9 8 7 6 5 4 3 2 1

To my husband, for always believing in me.
To my girls, for the joy (and chaos) they
brought to the process.

Contents

Introduction

EVEN BEFORE THE PANDEMIC, working across global offices required a different level of finesse than working with people you see every day. With work from home (WFH) becoming a new norm, we've added another layer to the difficulties of being an empathetic person in the office. How do we make the best of the situation we have in front of us: pixelated versions of the other human beings we rely on to get our jobs done?

I started writing this book as the novel coronavirus began. As curtains closed across corporate offices and employees from diverse fields were forced onto tools like Zoom and Slack—in some cases, for the first time— work from home became an overnight revolution.

Yet the need for a handbook to manage in the virtual workplace was long overdue. While the pandemic changed everything about office life, turning our living rooms into our backdrops via portals like Zoom, we were already living in a highly connected, always-on, virtual world. Most organizations had either adopted a global or virtual setup or had it on their agenda to do so. Employees increasingly requested it, so the pressure mounted on managers to learn how to make it work.

But doubts and questions surfaced—then and now. The best managers ask(ed) themselves:

- How do I make my team excited about working together if we can't ever see each other face to face?

- How do I increase engagement, retain my top talent, and coach others with no line of sight?

- How can I help those who are not aligned with the mission of the team when I can't meet behind closed doors or interact in person?

Since the WFH dynamic is here to stay, there is an urgent need for solutions to the problem of how to make it work for the long term—not as a Band-Aid until things change.

The mass switch to work from home for many white-collar workers around the globe comes with consequences. It effectively dehumanizes the people we spend most of our days with, turning them into two-dimensional people on the other side of the computer screen. Spontaneous interactions have been decimated, planned interactions have become drudgery, and everyone is searching for solutions to bring back the success from *humans forming teams and working together.* Our usual means of getting connection and intimacy at work may never return.

This situation may sound rather depressing, but that's not at all where I want to leave you. There is tremendous opportunity in and even an upside to this virtual world—where employees can better balance their work-life, the planet can be relieved of our commutes, and our talent pool can suddenly expand. But how can we communicate when the way we pick up on body language, word choice, and facial expressions has changed?

We have tools at our disposal to make virtual management the new norm—and a successful one at that. But doing so requires a fundamental understanding of one foundational element: *empathy.* In a work-from-home setting, empathy doesn't change at its core, but how we demonstrate it requires some special attention.

The information in this book is meant to help you cultivate *digital* empathy to effectively communicate, motivate your team, and influence others. In general, people focus on how the world affects them, not on how they affect the world. If even just some of the time you can turn the tables, it's an immensely powerful tool.

Given the cultural constraints that are still breaking down today, empathy shows the imperative of a different aspect of management—which has uses beyond the work-from-home setup. The macho culture we know so well, portrayed in the business press and across pop culture, focuses on *results,* not *people.* Many of the greatest management books that I hold in high esteem can come across as harsh or opaque in terms of feelings. That rhetoric or bias isn't relevant in the 21st century. The workforce is diversifying, capturing more talent from groups and mindsets that have been left out. This is the time to harness techniques that might be perceived as more feminine—*empathy* chief among them. While studies show that women tend to naturally be better at empathy, both men and women respond to training equally. Not to mention, to harness and promote diversity, it is critical to think about the perspectives of others who have been shaped by different experiences.

I'd rate myself as an empathetic person, verging on overly empathetic. I tend to focus on what others think about any one situation. I hope to take what comes naturally to me—my ability to put myself in another person's shoes and use that perspective to further my own goals, as well as theirs—to help you, the reader, find ways to achieve more in your work life using empathy.

In addition to my own empathy-driven insights, I share various examples I've seen in my global career. I've worked with remote teams for years—including for start-ups and esteemed organizations like *Financial Times*—as well as collaborated over videoconference, Slack, and WhatsApp.

In my time as a manager and as someone being managed, I've seen many scenarios where I thought putting aside one's own bias, even a small bit, and taking the perspective of the other person would have led to swifter resolutions, happier participants, and ultimately, more business value. Hopefully, the situations I lay out in this book can help people who don't naturally gravitate to that way of thinking learn to stop, check themselves, and explore other perspectives as an exercise in driving the greater good.

The goal of this book is to teach you to harness your digital empathy and learn skills to be a better boss, employee, colleague, and peer in a virtual or hybrid office. The real *how* of getting things done in an organization comes down to the people. And the best people at making things happen are the best at harnessing their empathy to connect and drive action.

Read on to discover how to refocus on what matters most, as you manage in a virtual-first world.

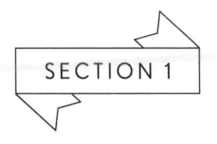

SECTION 1

MANAGING YOURSELF

How to Be More Empathetic, and How Empathy Helps You as a Manager

This book is meant to be both an explanation of how empathy can help you get ahead in a virtual office and a practical workbook, with tools to help you in common workplace situations. We start with managing yourself, because without putting yourself in your most comfortable, open-minded, empathetic place, you can't harness the tools required to understand others' perspectives. We then begin exploring empathy and how it can concretely help you in the office. Next, we cover your own emotions and how they affect those around you. And last, we discuss how to manage your own communication, so when you want to share things with people, they can hear you.

CHAPTER 1
IMPROVING YOUR OWN EMPATHY

What Is Empathy?

In my first job out of business school, I saw my manager just one time in my first year. One twenty-four-hour whirlwind business trip to New York together, and that was it for me to get an idea of who this man was, what he wanted, and how I was supposed to help him. In a fast-paced start-up, there wasn't much time for coaching or formal learning. We had things to do!

I paid careful attention on that trip and in all of our digital interactions later, knowing that my success at the company depended on our relationship. I parsed tone in emails, read body language from video streams of conference rooms, and gleaned insights into his behavior from coworkers. When he reads this paragraph, he'll probably also note that I made liberal, oftentimes *too* liberal, use of emojis in our frequent instant messaging.

It worked. Over our time together, we forged a strong, warm bond, where I knew what he wanted and why, often before he said it. Yet the number of hours we spent in the same room each year was minimal. How did I do it?

Empathy has been defined as "the ability to understand and share the feelings of another."[1] In its essence, empathy is how to be a successful human in a community, and it requires you to be able to envisage walking in someone else's shoes. This ability is what let me connect with this manager, despite our distance. *Digital empathy* is taking this skill and using it in a virtual environment.

People spend most of their time considering things from their own perspective, naturally. And now, we add to the mix the distance between colleagues working remotely, which makes them even less able to perceive each other's feelings and points of view. Changing that perspective is a key step in working well with other people. This is empathy!

I use the word *empathy* throughout the book for simplicity's sake, but I am really referring to *cognitive empathy*.

For many psychologists, there are three types of empathy:

- *Cognitive.* The ability to figure out what others are feeling and why

- *Emotional.* The ability to share the feelings of another, or vicarious empathy. You "catch the feeling."

- *Compassionate.* The desire to respond to or fix the situation affecting the other person's feelings

I want you to be able to better understand and utilize your ability to figure out what's going on in the other person's mind, without necessarily re-creating the emotions. Let's call it *perspective*, being able to circle away from your own point of view to see the situation from as many angles as possible. While you may not get to the "truth" of a situation, being able to speak and act in a way that acknowledges someone else's truth of the situation is an important step in reaching compatible conclusions for all parties. If you're having a disagreement with your boss—let's say they don't like the way you've allocated your team's resources—you're having an issue with perspective. Assuming you've put some thought and care into your allocation, your boss just doesn't see it from the same angle you do. Regardless of who's right or wrong, being able to figure out *why* your manager feels that way will help you make your manager feel heard, maintain your autonomy, and get to a solution that works for both of you. Seeing a situation from the other person's perspective makes everything easier.

I also want to make a key distinction, particularly as it relates to the workplace, between *empathy* and *sympathy*. The important part of harnessing empathy in the workplace is to understand others' feelings. You may not share them. And you certainly don't need to get to sympathy, which is an "understanding between people; common feeling."[2] If someone you work with is upset about something, say a new reporting structure with a new manager, you don't have to agree with them or *feel* the same way, but understanding how they feel, why they feel that way, and what that feeling sparks in them is key to relating better. It will help you both to achieve more, despite the circumstances they find unpleasant.

I once managed a woman who was extremely concerned with not repeating management mistakes that had been inflicted upon her—most notably, having a manager who had not helped her see a path forward with her role at the company. She was desperate to do things differently for her direct reports. A laudable goal. But I'd venture that she had trodden into the land of *ruinous empathy* (to be discussed in a few paragraphs). Understanding that her reports probably wanted to see this path for themselves was great; this is cognitive empathy, and it made her a great manager to them. But her desire to set up career steps for them came at the expense of their stated quarterly goals—which is what I needed from her first and foremost, for the business.

We'll come back to this woman later and how she and I worked through what would be a good solution for her, me, and her team.

Science says empathy starts with babies—children perceiving and then mimicking their parents' emotions, shown to them by facial expressions, tone of voice, physical gestures, and so on. This skill is a large part of what makes us human—communicating subtle emotional nuances. And empathy is a critical building block in molding human relationships, which in turn is a critical building block in a successful work environment, both from your and your employer's perspective.

A mentor once said to me that *getting stuff done in a corporation is easy!* (This man, I might add, was very empathetically minded.) He shared that you just had to harness the right people, get them all bought into your project, and keep them motivated. I think he meant this advice to be motivational, but to me, it just underscored the very complex nature of group work. Each of those three actions requires a complicated dance of wants and needs—including yours, the corporation's as a whole, and those of other individuals. Weaving them together is what people in senior leadership get paid the big bucks for!

Ruinous Empathy

I'd like to give a nod here to the work of Kim Scott and her book and theory, *Radical Candor*.[3] The book is a fantastic guide to giving feedback, but I think it's also given empathy a bad rap. Scott has a four-quadrant heuristic for dealing with people, with *ruinous empathy* being a result of being too kind to people, too careful of their feelings. This goes back to the three types of empathy and whittles empathy down to empathic concern, the desire to fix people's negative emotions. That is not my primary goal in using heightened empathy—to make your work life better and more enjoyable. Of course, not hurting people's feelings is often a good thing. But I completely agree with Scott that lots of terrible management stems from this type of empathy, which often encourages the least desirable behaviors. It is important to understand what people might be thinking, but then your actions have to suit you, your company, *and* the other person.

What Benefit Comes from a Focus on Empathy?

Studies have shown quite clearly that empathy in the workplace is positively related to job performance. Empathy makes you better at managing, being managed, and working crossfunctionally. Managers who show more empathy toward direct reports are viewed as better performers in their job by their bosses, a study from the Center for Creative Leadership points out.[4]

Empathy is tied to emotional intelligence, which many studies have proven makes people much better at their jobs. *Emotional intelligence* is defined as the capacity to be aware of, control, and express one's emotions, and to handle interpersonal relationships judiciously and empathetically. Multiple studies across the world have shown correlations between employees' emotional intelligence and their performance.[5] A salient example: a study in Germany suggests that people with better ability to recognize emotions in others have higher income.[6] If that's not an argument for honing your workplace abilities, you may want to consider a career that doesn't require these efforts.

Another way to think of the value of empathy in the workplace is from a team perspective. Google's well-known study Project Aristotle discovered that the main feature of a successful team is *psychological safety*. "Members of the team need to feel that they were safe to take risks, ask questions, or express their ideas without feeling embarrassed or rejected by their team members."[7] It comes down to an issue of trust. Do the people you work with trust you to take their perspectives into consideration when making decisions or taking actions? Do they trust you to communicate transparently?

Psychological safety should be the result of an empathetic and strategic leadership style. If you are able to put yourself in the team's shoes and modulate your choices with that information—to make the team feel heard and understood, while coalescing their efforts around a sense of unity—you are building toward psychological safety. Even if you have to make choices that displease some team members, approaching those choices in a straightforward, transparent manner builds a culture of trust.

But you and I don't need these studies to tell us what years of working in offices have made clear. When leaders try to take their team's perspective and then make decisions from that open-minded place, they are better for it, both for the quantifiable business results and the team's feelings. Most of the actions and efforts I've experienced or witnessed in the office that had a positive effect can be boiled down to an empathetic leader, or at least an empathetic perspective. And that's why I wrote this book—to help you learn, optimize, and utilize empathic skills and techniques to be better at work relationships and thus better at work.

What Is Empathy in a Virtual Workforce?

On top of these facts, we know intuitively that what is missing from a work-from-home (WFH) workspace is the human connection. Now, as the knowledge worker sector undergoes a dramatic change in style and function of work, it is time to be certain your skills are ready for this new reality.

Remote work both adds aspects to and removes them from our daily lives. On the one (positive) hand, WFH adds control to the commute; removes unpleasant interactions, like awkward chitchat in the bathroom;

and allows people to fit in workouts, laundry, or time with their family. And it gives people a stronger sense of autonomy, of having control over their own days. But it removes connection with colleagues in a lot of ways. We lose layers of trust, team unity, sense of purpose, creativity, and friendships.

As life has continued after the initial mass move to WFH during the pandemic, a new type of work location has emerged. Many people are blending working from home and working from the office: the hybrid solution. This development adds a layer of complexity beyond simply saying "everyone is working from home," as the balance of information and bonding in the office is shifted. Empathy will be a, if not *the*, key tool to balance people's desired locations and the community benefits and drivers of a successful office.

If you think about general life in an office, from the "olden days" pre-2020, it's easy to picture things about your coworkers. In an office, you get insights into coworkers' routines:

- Do they get their coffee at 10:00 a.m. on the dot every day or vary their routine?

- Is their desk cluttered or messy?

- Do they exude calm or excitement generally?

- What energy comes from being in the same room working on the same problem?

- How do they schedule their days on a set nine-to-five(ish) schedule?

- How do they dress and groom themselves?

In short, in a physical office, you can see a full picture of who they are and how they act, without even referencing the words they speak or the work output they produce. And a lot, though not all, is lost when we move to 100-percent virtual work. In a hybrid work environment, we gain some of this picture back, but it can be unbalanced. Those who are in the office are privy to these passive exchanges of information, while those who are fully remote may not pick up on these nuances.

What does this tell us? Virtual interactions change our ability to read people. If cognitive empathy is reading people's underlying thoughts, digital empathy involves translating those innate human perception abilities to the limited interactions afforded from virtual work.

What Does Empathy Bring to the Table?

What kinds of leaders do we need in this new hybrid workforce? If we assume that employees will split their time between working onsite and at home, we will continue to experience massive shifts in the way work is done. Work will inherently become more structured and asynchronous, to allow workers to do their best work while untethered physically to their colleagues. In this way, work will become more output-focused. The less people can "appear" to be working, the more everyone will be judged on numerical results, for better or worse.

But that doesn't mean human interaction in the office is dead. Far from it, as managers will have to unite their teams and direct their cumulative output to achieve results. And, you guessed it, the way to do this is to lead with digital empathy.

Leaders in this new world will need to walk that fine line between

- Focusing on the structure that allows for a great distributed work-force, in terms of output and efficiency
- Creating a work environment that causes people to believe in the effort and find enjoyment and rapport with their colleagues

We focus primarily on the latter in this book—building engagement through the *people* side of the organization.

We can assume that due to the diminished intimacy and opportunities to sense what others are thinking—thereby gaining understanding of their per-spective—in a virtual workforce, empathy is even more necessary. There's another way of looking at this: if you have less time to build rapport physi-cally with your team—to trust their work and acquire confidence that you are all on the same team—you will be more focused on the quality of their output. But more than ever, you will need to create opportunities to build trust. It likely won't happen naturally, with no physical environment for employees to "accidentally" interact and bond within. Managers will need to be connectors of their people—to create an environment where trust and safety can thrive.

Is it harder to get to psychological safety and team bonding in a virtual environment? Yes. As an example, during the pandemic, whistle blowing—that is to say, "ratting out" colleagues for illegal behavior, such as insider trading at the Securities and Exchange (SEC) commission—soared.[8] We can make a guess at this change in behavior: that some social glue was holding teams together, created by their presence in person. When you remove some of that glue, some of that feeling of team, people's allegiances change. They are no longer as committed to their employer, and thus, if their employer or some employees are engaged in illegal behavior, they are more likely to tattle.

Of course, fraud is a bad thing, so it's not a negative that there have been more whistle-blowing reports. But what about losing that allegiance and sense of camaraderie for positive business efforts? You can see how it's easier to check out and feel less committed to the common goals when you aren't face to face with the team day in and day out.

When we stop knowing *who* people are—including *how* they are day to day—we may only think about what they do for us. And while doing the work is crucial, if we measure people purely on output, they are more like cogs in a wheel, with a small avatar popping up on Slack every once in a while.

In a study at Penn State, researchers found that high-intensity telecommuting, defined as working more at home than in the office, had a negative impact on colleague relationships. The authors hypothesized that the "loss of 'face time' that comes with being a high-intensity telecommuter seems to bring deterioration of coworker relationships."[9] Intuitively, this outcome makes sense, particularly if the business and leadership are not making concerted efforts to mitigate the loss of relationship-building, trust-building, and intimacy-building opportunities. You can just look at the many studies aimed at social media that show how too much time looking at screens and pictures of people makes it harder to connect with people.

And dealing with other people and their emotions only digitally is almost certainly bad for empathy skills in humans. A frightening example of this comes from a UCLA study of a group of young teenagers at a summer camp, which found that those who used social media and spent a lot of time on screens were less able to recognize human emotions. The researchers "found that sixth-graders who went five days without even glancing at a smartphone, television or other digital screen did substantially better at reading human emotions than sixth-graders from the same school who continued to spend hours each day looking at their electronic devices."[10] The study group did not have access to screens of any kind, no phones or TVs, whereas the control group was allowed its usual amount. After five days spent interacting with their peers and camp staff, the study group improved their emotional and social engagement (e.g., tested by having to infer emotional states from photographs of facial expressions).

The ability to read facial expressions is key to understanding the perspective of others, and the fact that this is diminished in a digital world is something for all of us to understand and mitigate. In short, empathy is both learned and innate, and we as a society need to make sure we are working on maintaining those skills in our new virtual workspaces.

Mastering Your Own Emotions

The first key to being able to put yourself in your team's and peers' shoes is the ability to master your own emotions. You can't begin to take stock of other people's perspectives until you are in control of your own perspective. There are two facets to this ability:

- The first facet is *not allowing the emotions you feel to cloud your own judgment*. This is the topic addressed in other books and on many psychotherapists' chairs, so we look only at the negative ramifications of not mastering your own emotions as they relate to your ability to read people.

- The second facet is that *emotions are contagious and, if unchecked, negative emotions can spread like a virus among people you come in contact with, even virtually*. Everyone must work to not be patient zero in a collective bad work mood.

Why Being Emotional Makes You
Bad at Using Empathy

Emotions quite literally make us dumber.

When we experience negative emotions, unless we become mindful of what is happening and work to combat it, we lose our ability to engage in deep thinking. Our working memory is impaired, and, most saliently for this book, our ability to take someone else's perspective is dampened. Over-focusing on your own emotions can also bias you and cause you to lose your ability to home in on the problems and solutions for the business at hand.

The reason for this response stems from the fact that when we sense danger, our body prepares us to go into fight, flight, or freeze mode so we can protect ourselves. The prefrontal cortex, the part of our brain responsible for reading, math, and other deep-thinking tasks, is paused. While getting in a fight with your spouse or being sad your friends left you out of a group chat may not be the same as encountering a predator on the savannah, some of the same principles apply.

Scientific studies have looked at this phenomenon from a variety of perspectives, such as the idea that worrying and anxiety negatively affect working memory.[11] Another example, at the far end of the spectrum, found that depression can seriously hinder your cognitive faculties. One study from the University of Portsmouth compared hospital patients diagnosed with major depression to other individuals using several working memory tasks.[12] It found a statistically significant difference between depressed and normal individuals in a test that assessed working memory. It also found statistically significant differences between these two groups in tests that assessed central executive function, which includes directing attention, maintaining task goals, making decisions, and retrieving memories. For example, in a task that required participants to recall the last four letters of a string that varied in length from four to eight letters, the participants with depression had an average span of 3.2, but individuals without depression had an average span of 7.4.

In the most straightforward example for our purposes, a study from Wharton and Georgetown showed that anger literally hampers your ability to take someone else's perspective.[13] The researchers prompted people into anger and measured their ability to take other people's perspectives and found their abilities diminished, far more than in neutral or sad states. Thankfully, there is also good news. The researchers found that prompting individuals to correctly attribute their feelings of incidental anger moderates the relationship between anger and perspective taking. In other words, you can mitigate these emotions.

You need your brain to be functioning at a high level under the best of circumstances to read other people's behaviors and emotions—even more so in a virtual environment with limited signals.

Negative Emotions Are Contagious and Bad for the Team

Now that we've addressed how harmful negative emotions are to decision-making and cognitive abilities, we can see that an even bigger issue is that negative emotions are contagious. Anecdotally, you've probably seen that emotions spread like a virus; as we've discussed, one person's bad mood can put others around them on edge or in a foul mood themselves.

As mentioned earlier, psychologists call this *emotional empathy*, when you actually feel the other person's emotions with them, as if you had "caught" the emotions. Emotional empathy can also be known as *personal distress* or *emotional contagion*.

The authors of *Emotional Contagion*, experts in this field, define "primitive" emotional contagion as the "tendency to automatically mimic and synchronize facial expressions, vocalizations, postures, and movements with those of another person and, consequently, to converge emotionally."[14]

They argue that this happens in three stages: mimicry, feedback, and contagion. Primitive emotional contagion helps us coordinate and synchronize with others, empathize with them, and read their minds. These are both positive and negative, allowing us to bond with those around us—but also to affect them unwittingly. The unconscious mirroring of a companion's expression of emotion influences the perceiver to have a similar feeling, leading to emotional convergence.

Other academics back up this thinking in a work environment, such as the Schachter-Singer experiment in the 1960s, where participants watched colleagues complete a set of questionnaires.[15] The researchers measured the emotions of the observers in relation to the perceived emotions of the questionnaire takers. When the questionnaire takers responded angrily to questions, the observers felt angry in turn. But when the questionnaire takers responded happily, the observers also felt happy.

Another fascinating study out of Yale University put business school students into a role-playing management game but added a trained actor to convey one of four different moods: "cheerful enthusiasm, serene warmth, hostile irritability, and depressed sluggishness." The results revealed a significant effect of emotional contagion. Groups in which the actor had conveyed positive emotion experienced an increase in positive mood. Perhaps more importantly, these "positive" groups displayed more cooperation and less interpersonal conflict, and felt they'd performed better on their task than groups with the "negative" actor. And groups in which people felt positive emotions actually made better decisions within the confines of the management experiment. Interestingly but perhaps not surprisingly, when the students were asked why they thought their group performed the way it did, they made no reference to the idea that their behavior and decisions, and that of their group, had been directed by the displayed emotion of the actor.[16]

Negative emotions can additionally be compounded by complicated outside sources, such as a merger with unknown layoff possibilities, a bad economic forecast, or the departure of a great member of the team. In short, when possible, you want to do your utmost to limit the spread of your negative emotions to others. This is not to say you ought to be a robot, never feeling anything, hiding your true self away from your colleagues. Not at all! But there's a difference between allowing people to know what's going on with you and unconsciously dumping your bad vibes all over them.

One benefit we might have gained in a forced work-from-home environment: employees were less likely to spread their bad news if they were working alone, not seeing their colleagues. But alas, we know that this ability to catch emotions happens online as well. A 2018 study from Tilburg University in the Netherlands found that viewers readily catch the emotions of popular YouTube vloggers. When viewers see a positive post, they react with heightened positive emotions, and the same pattern holds true for negative posts.

Facebook data scientists tested emotional contagion by manipulating the newsfeeds of more than 680,000 users of the platform.[17] Some were given more positive posts and fewer negative ones, and others vice versa, more negative and fewer positive. After analyzing more than 3 million posts, the researchers found that people exposed to fewer positive words made fewer positive posts themselves, and those exposed to fewer negative words made fewer negative posts.

While emotional contagion relies mainly on facial and other nonverbal communications, it has been demonstrated to occur via text-only communications as well. People interacting through emails and "chats" are affected by another's emotions without being able to perceive facial or nonverbal cues. Take one study from Haifa and Johns Hopkins Universities, which showed that emotional contagion occurs even when nonverbal cues are scarce and only textual cues are present. Teams of coworkers were assigned a negotiation, and even using only email, "different behaviors are perceived as emotionally charged, resolute behavior interpreted as a display of anger, and flexibility as a display of happiness." And "that incongruence between text-based communication of (negative) emotion and emotionally charged behaviors elicits negative emotion in fellow teammates."[18]

It's important to focus on what you can do to mitigate this issue, because obviously, you can't always be in good spirits. And because of the limited interactions with people over videoconference and email, people may overthink smaller examples of moodiness. There's little chance of their overhearing you on the phone five minutes ago with your mother-in-law bickering about Christmas presents. Thus, they can't put two and two together to understand this is not a mood related to work.

To combat the negative emotions that we all feel at times, I've identified three ways to break the cycle:

1. Acknowledge

2. Put on a happy filter

3. Step back

ACKNOWLEDGE The first step is to acknowledge the fact that if you are down on yourself, you'll bring those around you down as well. Just remembering that can help you to put on a more positive face. I'm not saying you should bottle up your emotions. But there is room to take stock of a situation and proactively try to see it from a more glass-half-full perspective.

Being aware also means acknowledging your mood to your colleagues. In a Zoom world, you must be a bit more direct about your personal mood than you might have been in person. If you are in a foul mood, tell the people around you, "Hey, I'm having a rough day today. If I seem a bit gruff, it's not you." This statement can do wonders for people who are apt to think your bad mood is directed at them. It also shows you as a human being, giving you an opportunity to connect more deeply with those around you.

I'm not suggesting that everyone needs to know everything about what has brought you down. Taking this opportunity to share is not an invitation to whine and invite even more negativity. But honesty is, as they say, the best policy. A lot of headway has been made in the corporate world about taking mental health seriously, and showing that you take your own mental health seriously is a good indicator for your team. If you can, and if it's appropriate, take a mental health day if your mood is really foul and bound to bring down the rest of the group. And/or seek help from a professional if you need more support.

PUT ON A HAPPY FILTER Research has shown that you can turn some of this negativity around. Looking back at the Facebook newsfeed study, take advantage of these subconscious cues we are all influenced by, and look at some pictures or a comic or whatever would make you happy or put you in a positive frame before you write that email. You can also copy and paste text from emails you wrote when you were in a happier place to start your text from a neutral position.

As we saw earlier in this chapter, positive emotions are contagious too! In sports, when a team is generally upbeat, positive, and in an overall good mood, these positive emotions are "caught" by the individual players. And this is great for the bottom line. Results also show that when teams are happier, the athletes on the team tend to play better, according to a Sheffield University study.[19]

STEP BACK Lastly, if you can, step back from your computer when you're in a foul mood. The more you can do to both put yourself in a better state of mind and prevent the spread of those emotions, the better. Ideally, you'd do something to actually improve your mood—such as going for a run, meditating, dancing around your desk like a maniac—because we know that this negative mood is actually affecting your competence. But if you can't do that, the next best option is to focus on tasks that are solo work, so that you don't spread your mood. This option is a little like wearing a mask! Put a barrier up between you and your colleagues.

In this same vein, if someone you're working with is riled up due to an outside force, whether office related or not, it's best to try to dampen those intense emotions rather than amplify them. You want to find the right balance because, of course, if someone has a serious grievance, too much dampening can come off as downplaying their feelings; but at the same time, you don't need to amp them up.

You can compound people's emotions if you aren't careful about how you reflect back to them, and that won't lead to calm and clearheaded solutions. This is a great time to harness meditative techniques, step back, count to ten, and breathe. Ask yourself, "How does my attitude make this moment better?" You should give yourself time to process complex situations so that you can make sure your reaction will help those perceiving it.

The Best Communicating Starts with Listening

Listening is at the core of being able to understand others' perspectives. And being able to listen, both virtually and in person, is a key component of being a better leader. I like to break listening down into three parts:

- Taking in and digesting the information from someone's words
- Taking in and digesting the information that is *not* from their words
- Making them feel heard

If I had a nickel for every time someone equated empathy with listening, I would, well . . . have a lot of nickels. Much has been made about listening to people and how this is a major skill in management, and of course, it is. But I think it's reductive to focus solely on the word *listening,* because there are three ways to break this out that are beyond just the content of the words coming out of someone's mouth.

One is the real act of hearing. What are people saying with their words *and* with their tone, body language, and so on? You can't hear all the important messages someone is *not* saying with their body language, tone of voice, and word choices if you aren't actively listening to what they *are* saying. The second is their body language. What are their hands and face conveying, and are you picking up on those cues? Then there's the third aspect, the perception of listening. People want/need to be heard. If your speaker doesn't feel heard, then are you really listening?

Good listening is simply good management, despite it not being exactly empathy. Good listeners are more liked, rated as more attractive,[20] and garner more trust[21] than those who are not as adept at listening. Perfecting your listening skills should be an ongoing goal of any good manager.

The conflation between listening and empathy leads people to say that a good listener is necessarily empathetic, and specifically, that reflective listening with good eye contact means you are empathetic. I don't agree. These are good listening tactics; they are critical for making someone feel heard, but they don't

- Imply that you, the listener, understand the speaker's perspective or
- Make it easier to understand the listener's perspective.

These tactics are a type of crutch. They might make it easier to stay focused on important conversations, and they likely make the speaker feel more at ease—which in turn would cause them, hopefully, to reveal more—but they don't give you those additional data points you need to understand someone's true perspective.

Bad listening is, however, correlated with poorer social and emotional sensitivity. A study by Christopher Gearhart and Graham Bodie from Louisiana State found that undergraduates rated low in the quality they identified as *active empathic listening* (AEL)—a three-factor scale measuring listening across three dimensions: sensing, processing, and responding—had lower scores on a social skills inventory that measured, their ability to connect with their peers.[22] And conversely, studies show that effective AEL leads to increased satisfaction during business transactions.[23] See the endnotes for a link to the study by Gearhart and Bodie, or a quick Google search should lead you to the scale easily.

Practical Basics

Words are building blocks for humanity. Words allow information to be stably transmitted from person to person, across long distances. Phonemes (the smallest units of sound characterizing a language) are perceived faster than any other sounds by the human ears. We have evolved to talk and listen to each other.

To start, you need to hear the words the other person is saying. This is how information gets transmitted and, in a business situation, is critical for actually moving projects forward, being able to help your team solve problems, and understanding complex situations. Words are critical to how we communicate, yet just the tip of the iceberg in terms of listening.

Following are some basic listening principles that will help you hear the words the other person is saying.

BE PRESENT WITH YOUR EARS In a face-to-face world, being present means no laptop. If you're videoconferencing, that's hardly possible, but you can get rid of distractions and commit to being in the "room" for the conversation, not checking email, and so on. Everyone knows when someone has checked out of a Zoom call and is looking at their browser and not listening intently. If you care enough to take this call, make it worthwhile. In studies of students who were supposed to be learning in lectures, those who texted, emailed, updated their Facebook status, and sent instant messages had poorer grades than those who listened to lectures without distraction.[24] This finding aligns with the idea of *cognitive bottlenecks*; you can only process so much information at once before your learning starts to suffer.

UTILIZE MURMURS OF ASSENT A classic, much-noted listening technique is verbal and physical "murmurs of assent," like nodding your head and saying, "Yes, go on," or "I see." They contribute to the rhythm of the other person speaking while letting them know you are listening, at least enough to know where the pauses and moments of underlining (word choice) should be.

REFLECT IDEAS BACK Another classic method involves taking the time, when appropriate, to recap what the person has said. This technique has three benefits; two are basic, and the other is more advanced.

- The first is purely for the listener to know you're there and committed to the conversation.

- The second is to keep you there and committed to the conversation. It's hard to recap if you're not paying attention.

- And lastly, this is a tool for the speaker to gauge whether the words that are coming out of their mouth and into your ears are what they actually intend for you to hear.

Verbal communication has two parts: what the speaker thinks they are saying and what the listener thinks they are hearing. Often, they are not the same at all, as we've all seen in examples—like when someone says, "You're doing a great job, *but* you've missed these few things, and they are serious." And all the person hears is, "You're doing a great job."

This meeting of the minds is not a basic listening skill; it's, in fact, a very complex one. This skill definitely requires you to, in the moment, synthesize both the words and nonverbal communications, to be able to reflect back comprehensibly; for example, "You are saying that you are fine with the new reporting structure, but we've spent most of the conversation talking about the various drawbacks."

LISTEN TO NONVERBAL MESSAGES Be even more present with your eyes. This is a great example of why getting your own emotional house in order is important for being an empathetic leader. You need to be firing on all cylinders, so to speak, to see and hear the other cues people are giving you. While they are limited on a call or videoconference, it's still possible to pick up on distinct nonverbal communication. With someone you interact with often, it's good to ask yourself, "What is different this time?" Consider:

- Tone and pitch of voice.

- Pacing. How fast are they speaking?

- Facial expressions. Do their eyebrows, eyes, and lips say smiling? Or angry? Or sad?

- Word choice. How dramatic are their word choices? How negative/ positive?

- General energy. What's the general vibe they are giving off?

- Gestures. Depending on how much they usually talk with their hands and how much is visible in a videoconference, gestures can convey a lot about their energy. It's a classic, but sitting with arms folded is usually a sign of closing yourself off.

DETERMINE THE WEIGHTING OF THE TOPICS AND THE FOCUS OF THE CONVERSATION What subjects do they dive into, and what do they avoid? Probe these areas. As I mentioned earlier, imagine you are speaking to someone about their new reporting structure and they claim to be happy with it but spend most of the conversation talking about the various drawbacks. Often, people find it hard to stay off a topic that's bothering them, even if they aren't comfortable coming right out and voicing their dissent. This is one area where remote versus in-person communication doesn't play a big role, and thus, you can lean on it when you are not able to rely on nonverbal, physical cues.

LEAVE TIME AFTERWARD TO REFLECT AND TAKE NOTES For a busy leader, reflecting on what is said is the hardest. But so often, reflecting, particularly with pen and paper, helps you see things that, in the moment, you may have had trouble fully considering—but upon reflection, you can see well. The act of writing down these ideas also changes the way your brain sees things. You can and should also return to these notes for future conversations, particularly with important stakeholders and direct reports. Making sure you remember the conversation and opinions clearly, not just how your memory colors them in with time, is critical for making that person feel heard and understood.

Also, in a remote environment, you have fewer cues to remind you of situations, as each day has more similarity to the ones before and after it when you are at home. This makes note taking more critical.

How to Turn Listening into Empathy

In a great study, Jack Zenger and Joseph Folkman looked at what leaders in a coaching training program showed as listening skills and how they were perceived.[25] Similar to the ideas we've walked through, people are competent with the basics or at least understand what they are. But for the leaders to be ranked by the people they were coaching as good listeners, the answers changed. They flagged the following:

1. Challenging questions
2. Uplifting for one's self-esteem
3. Conversation flows in both directions
4. Making suggestions

This list aligns very neatly with my ideas on using empathy for listening. It's not so much the words, but rather how it makes the person feel. In my own research, very few people are willing to come out and say, "Positive feedback makes me think someone is a better listener." No one wants to be reminded flagrantly of their own biases!

ASK USEFUL QUESTIONS It's time to take a page out of a therapist's book and ask probing questions of the speaker. "What would you like me to do, how does this make you feel, what do you think they are thinking about this, and how confident are you about that? Could there be an outside force you aren't considering?"

BE SUPPORTIVE Mostly, people behave and think better when they feel positive about themselves. Criticism and negative thinking don't spur us to our best abilities to think and strategize. If you want your listening to leave a positive impact on the person speaking, you need to lace your listening with positive feedback and commentary, such as this:

- "I like how you're approaching this."
- "You're really well positioned to act on your thinking."
- "This is a solid strategy."

You don't have to lie, but there is always something positive to remark on, always a skill they could utilize to get through a complicated effort, and calling that out leaves the speaker with a halo of goodwill.

MAKE SUGGESTIONS Sometimes it is just better to validate and rephrase what a person is saying, as they are coming to terms with an idea. This approach keeps you from interpreting and bringing your perspective while the person is pouring out ideas or thoughts. But then, when it seems as though they have stated their situation or asked for advice, that is the time to offer advice and suggestions. The tone of advice and suggestions depends a lot on your role in their work, your own ability to be delicate, and how close you are to the problem. It's always better for people to come to solutions themselves, but sometimes you've been through a situation before and can offer concrete, useful suggestions.

TIME YOUR SUGGESTIONS . . . IN THE MOMENT AND LATER Good listening comes from good conversation. There are moments for suggestions while the conversion is going on. But it's also good to return to your suggestions later, after you have had time to reflect (see the next point).

RETURN TO THE IDEAS AT A LATER DATE Nothing says, "I was taking what you said seriously," like checking in later, concretely based on your notes from the conversation. This longer-term strategy helps define yourself as someone who listens—someone this person can trust with their ideas and thoughts.

In office conversation, there's also the spectrum of listening versus talking. In many instances, particularly coaching and mentoring moments, talking is the less advanced technique. Talking can imply you have to prove your point. There's nothing wrong with *having* to prove your point, but it's helpful to know when it's appropriate to be *trying* to prove your point.

Listening is what an advanced manager does. At a senior level, you should be getting paid to digest. Think. Feel. This is the soft power of *not* speaking: you have less to prove.

Other Types of Digital Listening

There are other great ways to listen that don't equate to conversations, such as data and surveys. The answer to what you can learn from people analytics technologies, like surveys, about what other people on your team and in your organization are thinking is both a lot and not very much, depending on your organization and approach.

Later in the book, I share an example of a colleague who was delighted that she had no negative feedback in her quarterly team survey. People didn't complain about anything. To me, this seemed like terrible news.

Obviously, there are different types of complaints in feedback surveys. But complaining that you want to be paid more, or that Marketing wants Sales to respect them more, is par for the course and very hard to permanently rectify. If people stop mentioning these issues, it means they don't care anymore or think their leaders can't or won't do anything to fix them. Basically, this lack of feedback equates to management purgatory. I would probably have to quit working and go hide in a hole if I stopped getting complaints like this, and ideally, I'll get more significant negative feedback. Serious feedback is a sign from your team or peers that they think you are the kind of person who wants to become better.

I think surveys have a very useful purpose for data in aggregate and for anonymous suggestions. They are also relatively easy and quantifiable, which is both a pro and a con.

Hopefully, you're enticed now by the idea of empathy and how you can use it to make your time more productive and communicative at the office. Putting these skills into use is easy for some and harder for others, but the payoff is immense. Without making a concerted change to be a better remote manager, you'll find it hard to achieve the same level of success you were attaining before the pandemic. A new world requires new skills. In the next chapter, we continue with the foundation: how to set yourself up to be your most empathetic self at work, through your energy, your space, and your interpersonal connections.

CHAPTER 2

FEELING GOOD WORKING FROM HOME

IN THIS CHAPTER, WE discuss how to set up work from home to work for you. You can't be a good, empathetic leader without getting your own house in order, both literally and metaphorically. We walk through some ideas on creating a work-from-home routine that can give you the energy, focus, and connection necessary for you to be the best leader you can be. And when you're energy is in the right place, you can foster connections with team members and colleagues that overcome the dehumanizing nature of remote work.

Manage Your Energy

What does energy have to do with empathy? We've covered a lot of this ground, but to summarize, your emotional state allows you to focus on others. Bringing your best self makes others feel good, and bad moods are contagious. Thus, in any environment, but particularly if you are at home and have potentially more control over your day, you should take advantage.

While I've often worked part-time from home, taking advantage of the flexibility to take more early-morning or late-evening calls as necessitated by a global role, it wasn't until the pandemic—when I tried to do a London-based job from San Francisco—that I was forced to really think about my energy in a work-from-home environment. And as we look to a hybrid workforce, being able to optimize location based on how it feeds your energies and competencies will allow you to be more effective. Every location—office, home, coffee shop—can be optimized.

Connect Your Work with Time and Space

Not unrelated to the discussion of energy, connecting with your work is about building your day and your space to create that same feeling of "I'm in the work zone" that an office gave you. One of the benefits of WFH is that it's allowed many of us to cut away a lot of the distractions that came from others being around us, not to mention the commute time, which frees up our schedules. Being cognizant of that and harnessing the hours in your days and weeks can lead to a lot of the gains that ought to come with working from home.

So what did we gain in an office? Neuroarchitecture, the study of architectural environments and their impact on the emotional and physical health of people, would say quite a bit.

What a Physical Space Gives Your Brain

There's an old joke: If the train station is the place where the train stops, then what is the workstation? In many places work itself had moved to open offices, where creativity was supposed to flourish. But, in my opinion, they were mostly just noisy. I had the (mis)fortune of being part of a business that moved to "hot desking," removing all ownership of desks so that in the morning everyone came in, plugged into a fresh workstation, and then left it completely clean (supposedly) and empty every night. The positives are that people can sit with a variety of teammates, learning more about how they spend their days. The reality is that this approach can also make the workspace cold, as you leave nothing personal overnight and choose a new seat in the morning. It also can lead to cliques if management isn't careful about demanding people be thoughtful about their seating choices. Not to mention finding desks in the morning can be a big waste of time if there's not quite enough capacity.

Generally, the office is designed for working, if not always in the most perfect or advanced way. A desk is relatively ergonomically designed for typing on a keyboard or writing notes, certainly more so than, say, working from bed. Conference rooms are definitely designed for the group work that they entail. Huddle rooms and smaller conference rooms can give privacy. All of this comes together to create a place where you know, intuitively, that you are supposed to sit down and work, both at your desk and collaboratively with others. A great home office setup should create the same situation for you.

Your environment affects your mental state. We know that in a traditional environment, light and temperature are critical to employee productivity and well-being. A study of office environments found the optimum indoor room temperature (69°F or 21°C) and illumination (1000lux) have improved the work performance, health, and productivity of office workers.[1] Even the decor matters! For example, in one study, college students were randomly assigned to different offices, where abstract or nature paintings were hung.[2] The students then performed four mild anger-provoking computer tasks and afterward reported their levels of anger and stress. Interestingly, this study was most effective for men, who experienced less stress with nature paintings. Findings from another study indicate that people who work in offices with plants and windows report that they "felt better about their job and the work they performed." This study also provided evidence that those "employees who worked in offices that had plants or windows reported higher overall quality-of-life scores."[3] This is all to say, your environment matters, and when you're working at home and have some control—children, spouses, roommates, dogs, and real estate constraints notwithstanding—you should work to make the best workspace you can.

What's your natural circadian energy like? Working from home allows you a lot more autonomy during your day, so being conscientious about scheduling both work and play (e.g., workouts, family and friend time, meals, focus work, and meetings) according to your own circadian rhythm can help you make your life as comfortable and productive as possible.

With that in mind, you should set up your calendar in a way that matches your energy. And in a way that matches your team at work. A woman on my team really wanted to use Friday morning as her "get shit done" time. But she was based in another country, several hours behind HQ, which meant she couldn't really use morning time for quiet, uninterrupted work. Blocking out her morning for "me time" took away too much of the limited time available for mutual workday phone calls. This team member tested out different scenarios, blocking free time in smaller and bigger chunks, to find the way that worked for her own energy preferences and for the rest of the team. In a hybrid office/remote model, you should plan your days to be in the office with people you want and need to be in the office with. Of course, for some meetings, it's obvious that anyone who can be in the office should be in the office. However, on some days, the people you want to connect with naturally gravitate to the central location, and you should take advantage of this opportunity for serendipitous connection.

Another facet of empathy is making decisions for the best of those around you. A team needs all members thinking outwardly for it to function optimally.

Given the solitude at home, productivity for some tasks is higher than at the office. So when you can, align your schedule to take advantage of this productivity. Which are your tasks that you need to hammer out or that require total peace and concentration? Save them for your work-from-home days. Make this schedule very clear to yourself and others via your calendar. I also like to schedule my international work on days when I'm working from home, since those calls would have always been over videoconference.

This way of scheduling frees up time in the office for more of the soft efforts that make work fun—having coffee with a coworker, going to lunch with a team, overhearing a salesperson pitching the product on the phone. A much-referenced study by Stanford economist Nicholas Bloom regarding Ctrip, a Chinese travel company, studied the productivity of workers at home and saw that they were able to increase productivity significantly for the tasks they were doing—mostly answering customer service calls.[4] More recent studies at Chinese tech giant Baidu show that, indeed, productivity does rise for certain, more formulaic tasks, but large-scale projects that require extensive teamwork, creativity, and ingenuity are, not too surprisingly, harder.[5]

Work Time Is Work Time

A problem with working from home is that there is no natural delineation between your workday and your home day. That oh-so-terrible commute actually serves a function: giving you time to switch from one set of goals and thinking (e.g., about your personal life, family needs, or your next vacation) to work mode. Without a commute and an office, you need to use your schedule as a blueprint to tell you what to do when. Otherwise, your time bleeds, you work longer hours than ever, likely with diminishing returns on productivity, and your emotional health suffers. This is not the behavior you want to model as a manager.

Research from Microsoft proves that our brains need breaks.[6] The study was clear: back-to-back meetings can decrease your ability to focus and engage. While we probably knew that intuitively, it's good to see the decrease in mental efficacy actually proven.

Another study from Stanford University and the University of Gothenburg shows the cause of Zoom fatigue is the length, number, and breaks between meetings.[7] It's critical to design a schedule that works for you and those on your team.

SET UP AN EFFECTIVE CADENCE When you're working with decentralized teams, managers, or direct reports, it's important to set schedules for communications, from weekly one-on-ones to biweekly Trello board sync-ups and assessments. Some people need external timelines more than others, but all of us need to add rhythms to the distanced work situation, fixed points in time that keep us anchored in the ups and downs of work-life.

Start with your own natural rhythms. Use a tracker and figure out when you're most focused on solo work, when you're most ready to chat and brainstorm with colleagues, and when you really need to take a moment to recharge. Look at your calendar with this goal in mind; you can even go so far as creating a private calendar only you can see mapped against these moods to better schedule your days. Then use this calendar to map out blocks of time when you'd prefer to have deep-focus time, meeting time, and personal time. Have your team do the same. While you can't meet everyone's needs, it's a good start to assess what each member's ideal schedule looks like.

PRACTICE GREAT MEETING HYGIENE We cover this topic in Chapter 7, "Distributing Knowledge Synchronously," when discussing how to run great meetings, but general meeting hygiene is important for keeping your day running smoothly.

BE TRANSPARENT WITH YOURSELF AND OTHERS What meetings do you actually need? A quarterly audit is a must, to cull meetings or participants that are no longer serving a purpose. Ideally, a meeting manifesto in your company's culture playbook would lay out why, when, and for how long you need meetings.

MAP OUT YOUR PERSONAL TIME IN ADVANCE To be able to advocate for yourself, it's also important to ask: What are your mandatory family and social commitments? And what are the things you'd like to do? Addressing these issues goes along with your natural rhythm as far as eating and workouts are concerned. Don't be ashamed to take time to eat lunch, work out, meditate, or clock out at 5:00 p.m. on the dot to see friends for a drink. Setting time aside in advance for these activities allows you to be more productive with the rest of the hours on your calendar.

As a last resort for protecting your time, schedule fake meetings. Yes, this advice is a little sneaky. But if you have a meeting that tends to run on and on with endless chitchat, it's okay to create a fake meeting directly afterward or even halfway through, to be able to confidently say, "I need to go now; let's get down to business and walk away with the action items or decisions we need from this time together."

Working from the office allows you to naturally close out your day with a commute, and I think it's important to artificially recreate this activity when you're at home. But even with a physical commute, deciding how to use that time, which can so often be wasted, should be approached thoughtfully. Do you want to use the time to decompress, entertain yourself, or socialize? Figure out what works for you; schedule it into your calendar so you can prepare by downloading the TV show you want to watch or planning a catch-up call with a friend. For WFH setups, this commute is even more important. During the pandemic, employees worked up to *three hours more* each day.[8] A clear start and end are critical in preventing this situation.

As a manager, you should give your teams these tools to make their own days work for them. One of the most consequential upsides of working from home is the autonomy it gives many workers. Allowing your team to make use of this independence will lead to happier people and more productive outcomes.

Connect with Your Colleagues

Being a human at work is about connection for many people. Friendships, romances, mentorship, even feuds and frenemies. For many people, a big energy driver at work is that feeling of community. How do you foster your own connections while working remotely?

During the pandemic, 75 percent of employees said they felt more socially isolated, 57 percent felt greater anxiety, and 53 percent felt more emotionally exhausted.[9] And more than half of employees said they felt lonely while working from home, according to a survey by Blind, an anonymous professional network.[10] Connecting with your colleagues is a key attribute of employees who feel connected to their work.

Why WFH Is Dehumanizing

Anyone who's ever been in a large Facebook group or Reddit forum can tell you how quickly people devolve into making offensive statements, stereotyping, and dehumanizing others in online forums. The anonymity afforded by being online allows you to be less empathetic. This lack of connection plays out across all our virtual interactions.

There are many studies covering the dehumanization of virtual connections. The most vivid for me actually comes from the art world. The artist Wafaa set himself up in a gallery in Chicago. He gave the internet the opportunity to point a real paintball gun at him. He was inspired by the military's use of drones and how a pilot in the US could wield a drone to cause death and destruction, yet feel so removed from the situation, like a video game.

Some people were unsurprisingly awful, trying to hurt him and destroy his living quarters. The cloak of anonymity allowed these random people on the internet shooting at Wafaa to act without empathy. I don't imagine your colleagues doing *exactly* this, but this type of behavior can be extrapolated to all virtual interactions.

Beyond art exhibitions, studies have looked at dehumanization in office behavior. One study by Juliana Schroeder, Michael Kardas, and Nicholas Epley had people either listen to or read a transcript of people explaining their opposing political views.[11] Study participants were then asked to rate and describe the person whose views they had read or listened to. Reading the transcripts led the participants to dehumanize the author far more than watching a video or listening to an audio file of the same words. The subjects found their counterparts "mindless," as opposed to holding intelligent thoughts about the matter at hand.

If you aren't face to face with someone, you may think of and ultimately treat them as less of a person than those in front of you. This behavior is critical when thinking of how you work in a remote context, particularly with people you have never met. Fight every possible urge to think of them in a two-dimensional fashion. It's really important to create a three-dimensional relationship as best as possible, so you can understand and relate to them in an emotional context. This way, you can read their cues beyond the words coming out of their mouths and the limited facial expressions you can see.

Communication That Drives Connection

The only way to decrease this dehumanization and perceived distance between you and those you work with is to enhance your communications. There's a spectrum of human communication, from in-person to text-only. In-person, one-on-one communication is multilayered—from body language, hand gestures, tone of voice to pace of speaking. Clearly, a text message can hardly compete.

One of the biggest issues with work from home is the weakness of video-conferences as a way to connect with your colleagues, yet it seems to be the best tool we as a corporate society have to connect better. While it may feel like this connection is richer, a lot of that is an illusion. And this collective commitment to video may not be a good thing. From a study at Carnegie

Mellon's Tepper School of Business, the authors found "that video conferencing can actually reduce collective intelligence. This is because it leads to more unequal contribution to conversation and disrupts vocal synchrony. Our study underscores the importance of audio cues, which appear to be compromised by video access."[12] There are two main issues with a videoconference as a tool for digital communication: it's draining, and it's conversationally inefficient.

Zoom Is Draining—How Can We Change That?

Everyone knows long Zoom days are exceptionally tiring. Looking at yourself is extremely draining. It's as if you're doing an entirely different task at the same time as trying to participate in the meeting. If you're not looking at the people in the call because you're presenting, you're suddenly an actor in a play, performing on a virtual stage. This is tiring as well.

Think about what you can and can't see in a videoconference. In a normal meeting, you can pretty much see only the person you're looking at. In a videoconference, you can also see much more in your "peripheral" vision because it's all on the screen in front of you. So everyone's face is within your line of vision. This setup is terrible for most humans; it can be really overwhelming and tiring. Your brain is working overtime on Zoom to create the same flow of information that it was accustomed to in an in-person work environment.

Online attention is of a different quality, making us overly focused on the few available visual cues that we historically gathered from a full lexicon of body language. On a video chat, we need to work harder to process nonverbal cues. Paying more attention to these cues consumes a lot of energy. Our minds are together when our bodies feel we're not. Not only does the effort require more energy, but that dissonance, which causes people to have conflicting feelings, is exhausting.

Lastly, these calls are draining because they involve so much sitting. Do anything you can to counteract the physical drawbacks of videoconferencing all day. You must get up, stretch, practice chair yoga, wear blue-light glasses, or invest in a standing desk. Anything you can do to keep your body from stagnating in front of a screen. It's not good for your health, and it's not good for your thinking.

How to Make Zoom Less Draining

- *Do you even need video?* Maybe a phone call is enough.
- *Walk and talk.* When appropriate, take calls while walking, which is good for your energy levels and opens up different parts of your brain.
- *Change your view settings.* Gallery view means you're working overtime to register all the faces, which is exhausting; focus on the speaker. (Or someone else! Zoom does allow you to covertly read other people's reactions.)
- *Don't look at yourself.* Take a sticky note and cover up your own face.
- *Schedule breaks between calls.*

Conversational Inefficiencies

One of the most difficult aspects of video calls is that they break up our natural speaking gaps and overlaps. These are different from culture to culture, but American English involves a lot of overlaps, and any lags in conversation make people uncomfortable. The delay in virtual communications and also in telephone calls, particularly when more than two parties are on the line, can be detrimental to the flow of the conversation. Studies have shown that this delay, even though it's not the speaker's fault, leads to the perception that the other person is not listening.[13] This is a very important fact for our new virtual world, at least until videoconferencing and broadband technology improve to a degree that it's not. There's also an extra layer of confusion: what's being communicated versus what's a digital hiccup? Sometimes, if others are silent, you think, "Oh, did you freeze? Are you still there?"

There is an upside, though. Because we are used to overlapping conversations and interruptions, they are considered signs of a vigorous and positive conversation. But this way of communicating also favors people who are gregarious and comfortable with this behavior. By eliminating that possibility and having to build structures to create the flow of the conversation, such as hand raising or using turn-taking tools in videoconferencing software, we enfranchise people who may not have felt as comfortable before. This way of behaving increases diversity of thinking, which is always beneficial.

ZOOM TIPS What's the best strategy to not get railroaded by people who hog the floor?

- *Insist on taking questions at the end of the call.*

- *Make use of the chat function in your videoconference tool.* If that's how you want to poll people, decide who will speak next or find other ways to communicate along both channels simultaneously.

- *Utilize virtual hand raising.*

- *Nominate someone to take notes and follow up with written documentation.* Make sure this workload is equitable, though I must admit, there's a secret power in being in charge of the note taking and making sure everyone knows the action items at the end of a meeting.

- *Use a separate thread for questions, such as Slack or sli.do.*

Other Ways to Humanize Work from Home

We cover a lot of bonding activities in Chapter 4, "Driving Real Connection with Your Team," but generally, there are two important categories for humanizing remote office life. One is making yourself a human for your colleagues' benefit. And the other is making it easy to see your colleagues as human.

Make yourself easy to approach and open. This is the foundation of a work environment where everyone feels as if they know and value their colleagues. Bring your whole self to work. Doing so takes practice, to find balance between getting offtrack talking about personal stuff and letting your colleagues in on your inner workings. But much like we discuss in the section on the contagion of moods, being up front about where you are emotionally and why is both humanizing and useful to your colleagues.

In many ways, WFH is better for this behavior, as everyone can see each other's bedrooms, dogs, and how many times a day the Amazon delivery person rings the bell. There's an inherent intimacy. It shouldn't be hidden, though obviously, limiting distractions is key to getting work done. This means leaving time and valuing chitchat. I think it's useful to be explicit and say, "We are chitchatting," even using an icebreaker or a more "formal" way of chitchatting, like saying "Everyone share what they had for lunch." This explicitness reminds people of the purpose of informal information sharing. It's not about wasting their time. It's about connecting them to their colleagues so they can feel as if they are part of a team and enjoy work more.

Make sure your messages have warmth to them, when possible. This topic is covered in more detail in the "Written Comms: Emails/Slack/Doc Commenting" section in chapter 3, but actively trying to inject warmth into your communications can go a long way toward creating a human environment. See also the "Creative Communication" section in Chapter 3, where we cover emojis. :)

From an external standpoint, the number-one thing you can do is focus on the great things your team and colleagues do. Our negativity bias as humans causes us to focus more on the flaws in people and situations. By praising others, just quietly to yourself, privately to them, or publicly, you combat this thinking. Studies show that describing someone's good attributes increases both their happiness and confidence.

It's also critical to create an opportunity to connect when something seems off. Ask yourself, "Am I paying attention to changes in behavior within my team? What about personal problems?" Sometimes, people's personal lives invade their office life; this is a part of being human. From trying to conceive a baby to the death of a loved one, some life events or passages are all-consuming and can change someone's attitude or performance. These are very tricky moments to manage, walking a line between being a caring human being (which you should try to be!) but also not straying from what is professionally appropriate for the person you are dealing with. And that boundary will be different for everyone.

When you think something is up with a direct report, colleague, or manager, ask yourself, "Has their attitude changed dramatically? Do they look exhausted for weeks on end, like maybe they have been crying? Or have they started being absent, when that was never an issue before?"

How do you broach the topic if you are concerned about a team member? Gently, privately, and lightly. They may want to tell you exactly what is going on. Then, it's a key time for empathic listening. Or they may only allude to the issue. You want to err on the side of kindness, particularly if you've worked with them for a while and you know this behavior is out of character.

You can ask yourself, "How would I like to be helped?" This is a time to really consider empathy. But are you very similar to the person? That may not be the response they want. I think the least you can do is open the door for discussion and understanding, but be respectful of their privacy. In practice, this approach might mean asking them to stay on the line after a team meeting and asking if anything is going on. You can mention they seem a bit blue, down, out of sorts. Your communication really needs to come from a place of concern and not as a performance question, so it's crucial not to give examples of where their behavior is impacting work, but merely that their human side is coming through and that it's a different side from the one you've seen in the past. Make sure to frame this behavior as an event, a passage through something, not a "problem" (e.g., having a child is not a "problem"; it's just a mix of personal and professional and a change in circumstances).

Sending an email later is okay, leaving the door open: "I don't want to make a mountain out of a molehill, but I've noticed you seem a little out of sorts. If there's anything I can do to make the work side of your life better, please let me know." This has nothing to do with you—most likely!—and you don't need to insert yourself into their life, but you should appear to be open to helping them.

Occasionally, perhaps quarterly, you should mention that your "door" is always open to discussing things that might be affecting people's moods, as you may not be able to spot differences in behavior over the phone or on Zoom.

In this chapter, we covered how to humanize our colleagues and how to energize our work days and spaces. Ideally, armed with your listening skills, you're now ready to feel as if you're really putting these skills into action. The next test of harnessing digital empathy is presenting yourself online—being the best avatar of yourself at work so that you can, in the words of the great Dale Carnegie, win friends and influence people.

CHAPTER 3

"SPEAKING" SO OTHERS WILL UNDERSTAND

Communication Overview: The Substance and the Method

How do you deliver your messages differently in a Zoom-first world? We cover the tactics of sharing information in Chapter 6, "Distributing Knowledge Asynchronously," but first, let's tackle how to approach conveying these messages—and specifically, how *empathy* can help virtual communications land more effectively. We walk through three ways to look at communications:

- What you are conveying just by existing

- Which types of communications are ideal for different purposes

- How to make sure your messages translate across cultures

The lack of in-person communication changes humans' natural abilities to read more than just each other's words. We now have many more channels through which to communicate—Slack, email, videoconference, phone, Trello boards—which is both an opportunity and a challenge.

With more than just face-to-face communication to navigate, you need to dismantle what is behind your messages—and become intentional about conveying them. Being thoughtful about how your actions impact the recipients of your messages can help others perceive you as smarter, nicer, insert-desirable-adjective-here, and more convincing. In other words, there is a strong personal and professional ROI from getting your communications right.

Your Actions and Choices

Everything you say and do conveys information. An ideal manager in a remote role would harness this vast amount of communication information to make their desired points, but that doesn't always occur. Many defer to the communication style they know best and are most comfortable with.

Despite our best intentions to not judge a book by its cover, superficial impressions mean a lot and can persist for years. And in the virtual setting, most of the split-second judgments people make about others happen through a 15-by-10-inch screen. That's very little real estate for telling all the stories that we used to tell people in person.

People are learning about you from your physical self, your voice, and your work environment. Thinking about these elements can help you to convey the stories and ideas you want to convey.

A caveat: We might ask ourselves, "Is this how the world has to be? Do we have to be judged on the attractiveness of our voice or the tidiness of our office?" I can hardly be the arbiter of such a weighty societal question, so my opinion is to err on the side of the traditional perspective. Do you have to display a pleasant voice or neat demeanor to succeed? Absolutely not. Might it be easier if you do? You betcha! If you're going to buck convention, at least be aware you are doing it and understand the potential impact it might have on how other people perceive you. The goal of using empathy, as I said at the beginning of the book, is not to actually *feel* what others are feeling, but to be able to understand what they are feeling and act with that knowledge. The same applies to these superficial traits: it is useful to anticipate how others may respond to your communication choices, so you can select the most effective approach. This chapter presents best practices for communicating with digital empathy during the workday.

YOUR PERSON Don't waste the opportunity to tell the story of who you want to be in the office. Just because you can go to work every day wearing just your underpants on the bottom doesn't mean that we've entered a utopia where looks don't matter. They still do. And you can't do too much about how you look, but to pretend appearance doesn't matter is naive and wishful thinking.

Studies such as psychologist Edward Thorndike's work in the 1920s—with commanding officers evaluating soldiers based on their looks—led to an idea known as the *halo effect*,[1] which is the tendency for positive impressions of a person, company, brand, or product in one area to positively influence one's opinions or feelings in other areas. In Thorndike's study, commanding officers scored soldiers in terms of physique, bearing, or voice, and those they scored higher in these superficial categories were likely to be scored higher in qualities such as leadership and loyalty. And the inverse was true as well; soldiers who were rated as below average on one quality were often rated as below average on all the others.

Your apparel also makes a difference in how you are perceived. In a study from NYU/Princeton, the authors looked at how *economic status cues can affect our perceptions*.[2] They showed community members and undergraduate students pictures of random faces matched with cheap or expensive tops. They asked the participants to judge the competence of those in the images. The result? Faces paired with more expensive clothes were judged as more competent, even if the participants were explicitly told to disregard clothing in their judgments of competence. Clothes matter! But yes, in this Zoom world, don't bother investing in great trousers!

Everything you wear in the office tells a story. I could tell you that *you should just be you* and that the people who care about these things are shallow, but that would do you a disservice. You don't need to diligently follow a corporate dress code, even if that is sneakers and hoodies, but it's best to be thoughtful when you can about your appearance, to make sure you are telling the story you want to tell. If you don't care at all about clothes, then you should enlist help. Find a uniform and formula that work for you, and stick to it.

Your facial expression matters too! In another study, participants were asked to pick faces that they wanted as their financial advisor out of a lineup.[3] Despite happiness not being a core trait of a financial advisor, participants picked the happy-faced advisors more often. Though eye contact is harder to achieve given current videoconferencing technology and camera angles, it's important to remember that eye contact makes you appear more intelligent (this also applies back in the office). Research has shown that bystanders watching a video of two people conversing consistently rate those who make more eye contact as more intelligent.[4] If you can, look in the direction of the camera as much as possible. This makes it hard to see people's faces and reactions, so you're trying for your best, not perfection. Also, set up the Zoom squares so that they are centered below the camera and you aren't always looking to the left or right. It's obvious that someone has two screens when they aren't paying attention, and you see this behavior all the time. Investing in a cheap camera to put above your larger screen easily fixes this issue and gives the impression you are paying attention.

There are a million reasons to try to get good rest, and here's another. Other small appearance factors can hinder you. Tiredness is perceived as less attractive. Open eyelids are considered more intelligent, and thus droopy, tired eyes are seen as less intelligent.[5] Try to keep your face friendly and smiling. Going around grinning like an idiot won't help if that's not your natural proclivity, but it's well known that a smile makes you more attractive. And a smile is very clearly visible on camera.

You should also think about how smaller behaviors become a part of the personality your colleagues associate with you. Some behavior cues that communicate a message to those who see them are subconscious, such as

- Are you frenzied or relaxed?
- Do you speak loudly or quietly?
- How do you approach meetings and introductions?

A new hire in my organization came to every meeting late in his first two to three weeks. Why? I was watching from my desk. He wasn't coming out of other meetings late. Showing up late seemed to be just his natural timing. What would this habit say to your new colleagues? It sends a message that you don't want to be on time. Particularly in a culture with thirty-minute, back-to-back meetings, not being productive and present in meetings is a waste of people's time.

This employee also kept his laptop open and typed and moved his mouse around during meetings. We didn't have a *laptops-closed* meeting culture, so this behavior was not verboten per se; but it was also clear that he wasn't taking notes or something similar. Maybe there are reasons to portray yourself as *too big a deal* for the meetings you are in, but it's a very high risk to be so cocky. And I found myself doubting he was making a conscious effort to think about what he was trying to project. That is where the risk really lies— inadvertently telling stories with your behavior to all your new colleagues, without thinking what those stories convey.

Besides behaviors like showing up on time and demonstrating your full attention, is your body contributing to what you want to convey? Hand gestures are significantly muted and can be distracting in a video call, and thus need to be considered and likely practiced. Videoconferencing usually falls somewhere between a large audience and a small one, when you think of how to use your hand gestures—a new context for human gestures. If you sit 2.5 feet away from your screen, there's a bit of room for your hands, but others can read your face. Recording yourself and watching your hand gestures to see where they are falling within the screen and if they are distracting can be helpful.

Don't let your face go slack. Nodding and head tilting give the impression of listening. How far should your face be from the screen? Your face should take up no more than one-third of the screen. Take a cue from Instagram influencers: your face should fill somewhere between a quarter and a third of the screen and no more.

If you are in a conference room setup, don't get lazy about your body language. I remember having a promotion discussion with a man on my team over videoconference. Because he was in the office and his camera displayed the whole room, I found myself looking at a man sitting splayed out like he didn't care at all about the outcome of the discussion. Did he realize we could see that? It's good to understand what the camera shows, but it's better to just assume others can see everything and therefore position yourself accordingly. I can say that the body language was certainly not a great tactic in his negotiation to get promoted. You should always be sitting professionally. Lean, but don't hunch; this is where a real desk and setup can be very helpful. The foundation helps you sit normally, with feet on the floor. This advice will also be important in a hybrid setting, where most likely, people will be watching the conference room on video.

YOUR VOICE Your voice is a critical medium for delivering your message. In a study from the University of Chicago, MBA students were videotaped giving pitches on why they should be hired. Then, potential employers and professional recruiters were given three options: view the video, listen to the audio, or read a transcript.

The result? "These evaluators rated a candidate as more competent, thoughtful, and intelligent when they *heard* a pitch rather than read it, and as a result, had a more favorable impression of the candidate and were more interested in hiring the candidate. Adding voice to written pitches, by having trained actors or untrained adults read them, produced the same results. Adding visual cues to audio pitches did not alter evaluations of the candidates. For conveying one's intellect, it is important that one's voice, quite literally, be heard."[6] Your voice, with its many layers of communications mechanisms, honed over millennia, is an exceptional tool for conveying your message.

Speech patterns—including your accent, tone, speed, and pitch—paint a very vivid picture of you for the people you encounter. According to a study by William Apple, "comparing recordings of speakers that were artificially enhanced to be slower or faster, if two speakers use the same words, but one speaks faster and louder and with fewer pauses and greater variation in volume, that speaker will be judged to be more energetic and intelligent"[7] Paying attention to your voice, particularly when phone calls have increased in importance, should pay dividends.

Pitch—how high or low the sound is—is the voice-related concept most discussed in terms of business outcomes. A high sound has a high pitch, and a low sound has a low pitch. A tight drumskin gives a higher-pitched sound than a loose drumskin. At Duke University and the University of California, the speeches of the male CEOs of almost 800 public companies were studied. CEOs with deeper voices managed larger companies and had higher income. A decrease of 25 percent in voice pitch (22.1 Hz) is associated with an increase of $187,000 in annual salary. Additionally, CEOs with deeper voices also enjoy longer tenures.[8] This connection between lower pitch and success is thought to be evolutionary. Many of our closest animal relatives, from rhesus macaques to chimpanzees, lower their vocal pitch during altercations.

Does the same hold true for women? Somewhat. Traditionally "female" ways of speaking—using a sing-song tone of voice, speaking in a breathy way, or ending sentences in a questioning tone (often referred to as "upspeak")—can be seen as less intelligent and authoritative. And studies have shown that lowering pitch is as effective for women as for men. In an experiment at the University of Illinois at Urbana-Champaign, participants performed a decision-making task that involved ranking the items that an astronaut would need to survive a disaster on the moon. Afterward, the researchers privately asked each participant to rank each member's dominance, creating a pecking order for the groups. Most participants quickly shifted the pitch of their voices within the first few minutes of the conversation, and those changes predicted their later ranking within the hierarchy. For men *and* women, participants who lowered their pitch were perceived to be more dominant, and those who raised their pitch were seen as more submissive.[9]

That said, there's also a lower limit for women—called *vocal fry*, the sound of insufficient airflow—that is penalizing. A study at the University of Miami found that having a deep voice characterized as *fry voice* (most easily recognized in imitations of Valley girls, but YouTube also has many good examples of what this sounds like in practice) could be a hindrance for women, causing employers to view them as being less educated and competent.[10] Vocal fry is another reason to slow down and keep breathing while speaking to colleagues. In short, everyone needs to find the pitch that works for them, but generally, lower is better.

Pace of speech is also important. While faster speakers are perceived to be more credible, according to a study,[11] you don't want to speak so fast as to be unintelligible. The ideal speaking rate is about 150 words per minute.

In this world of remote work and Zoom presentations, taking steps to improve your voice can go a long way. A great first step to learn about your speech is to record yourself and take a long listen, maybe with the help of a kind yet critical friend. You have to work very hard to recognize and then rectify speech patterns, so this effort might be worthwhile only to correct something that really sticks out and grates. But it's worth at least taking realistic stock of what you're working with. Here are some actions that may help:

- Record yourself speaking freestyle, particularly for identifying pitch and fillers such as *um* and *ah*.

- Hire a speech coach.

- Join a club, like Toastmasters.

- Test out AI-driven tools, such as Speeko, which is an app that trains you to improve your diction, pace, and so on.

- Practice reading passages aloud and timing yourself, aiming to hit that 150 words-per-minute goal.

- Use tongue twisters. Strengthening your speaking muscles will help you have more control when you're in a stressful situation.

- Insert words in a passage when reading out loud, to practice slowing down and thinking about your diction. You can add *and* after every word when reading a passage out loud. This will force you to read without thinking what the passage means. The phrase "she sells sea-shells by the seashore" becomes "she and sells and seashells and by and the and seashore."

One closing thought on speech modification comes from a story about Margaret Thatcher. As England's first female prime minister, she worked hard to lower the tone of her voice by an astonishing 60 MHz. But for most listeners, her efforts didn't work. Her speech appeared false to her counterparts and diminished her credibility. And therein lies the secret: while you can make improvements, you don't want to lose yourself in the process. People can smell falseness a mile away.

YOUR PHYSICAL SITUATION So much of your physical setup has been covered since the pandemic began, but it's important to set yourself up for success. Consider what people can see beyond your face and body, starting with the infamous background. Wear it like an accessory! Everyone's watching to see what your "at work" behavior says about you. The nonverbals of an organized and streamlined setup send a strong first impression. Importantly, how you present yourself through your setting has the power to remind your colleagues that you are just as committed to the relationship as if the meeting were happening in person.

For better or worse, people are taking in your background and making judgments about you. I once interviewed a woman and spent the entire hour wondering if there was a hologram behind her chair due to a trick of the eye and her oddly chaotic background. She didn't get the job because it wasn't the right fit. But would she have had a better chance if I hadn't been so distracted? Probably.

As I'm writing this, I hate the stock digital backgrounds available on Zoom, Google Hangouts, and the others—generally. I find them distracting, turning us even more into two-dimensional avatars of our coworkers and focusing my attention on what they are hiding. As the technology improves, and I'm sure it will, I may change my mind on this issue. Privacy is important, but sometimes seeing part of people's homes can build relationships or start conversations. I have a funky piece of art behind where I often sit on informal team calls, and it always provokes comments. I don't have to sit there, but it can be nice to have something to talk about.

If you can make it happen, sit in a well-lit, clutter-free workspace with just enough personality to make you human yet not too much as to provide a distraction.

Your Communication Tools

We have a plethora of ways to communicate while working remotely, and that number of options is likely to increase in the future. Each tool, from the old-fashioned phone call to the as-yet-uninvented group chat avatar feature, has pros and cons and should be used with its context and limitations in mind.

Written Comms: Emails/Slack/Doc Commenting

Slack was invented to replace email. I've not personally experienced that benefit, but maybe you have. The two platforms have a lot in common. Slack and emails are both searchable and persistent, and you decide who receives your message. Using these platforms leads to some guidelines—such as the classic *who, what, where, when, why,* and *how* of journalism—for making sure your messages reach your teams' and colleagues' "ears" effectively.

Who? Be mindful of who is intended to see the message and who *could* see the message. Messages get forwarded; we all know this. And conversely, are the people you're including necessary? No one likes a cc: spam.

What? Always make sure you have a point and that the point is clear. If there's a summary, lead with it. Make it easy on your reader to assess your main message and meaning.

Where? Is this venue—for example, a teamwide email, a one-on-one Slack, a message to most of the team—the most appropriate for this message, given when people will receive it and the necessary formality or informality? This is a particularly good question to ask when considering Slack channels that may have a multitude of members. Ask yourself, "Is this the right place to post this message?"

When? Consider the asynchronous situation and when people will read what you send.

Why? Before sending any email, it's worth asking, "Why am I sending this?" Then, let your recipients know. If there's an action needed, spell it out.

How? How well did you craft your message? At the heart of it, what's the nicest and simplest way to get your point across? As discussed previously, negative emotions are contagious in written work. A good life rule: don't be a jerk over email. And proofreading says a lot about how seriously you take what you're writing.

As important as what you *do* say can be what you *don't* say. What kinds of things do you not want to write down?

- Rude things
- Criticism

- Things people will stew over

- Illegal things (This should go without saying, but you never know!)

Things you do want to write down:

- Action plans

- Praise—direct or indirect

- Things you *do* want people to stew over

I've spent a good deal of my career as an email marketer and have thought a *lot* about what to put in the subject and body of an email to get people's attention and inspire them to take action. And the key tenet of email marketing is to *think what your customer wants or needs to hear.* You need to put yourself in the recipients' shoes to make your communications worthwhile.

A prime example of *not* putting yourself in the recipients' shoes is the phrase "see below." This is so lame. You, the writer, already know what is below and what you want the reader to take from this email. So summarize! "Bob, see below for Jenny's thoughts on the new launch timeline, which really concerns me. I think ninety days is the fastest we can do. I'm going to bring this up in our call this afternoon, and I wanted to run it by you in advance. Full details below." Now, Bob doesn't have to see below. He can, if he wants to dig deeper. But he can also quickly become apprised.

This method of considering your readers and being respectful of their time in reading, to me, is key in upward emails—that is, in emails to senior people you want to impress. Make your email both quick and efficient to get the basic idea, but also give room for digging deeper.

I started my career at a French fashion house with a very strict email hierarchy, and this taught me a lot about being

- Extremely polite in email and

- Very succinct when emailing very senior people.

When you want to send someone an article, of course, you send the link. But why not also quickly copy and paste the text (particularly the relevant parts) if doing so is easy, so it's already there for them? Particularly if the person you're emailing travels a lot or is in a lot of meetings, you're sparing them the steps of clicking through, being bogged down by ads, and so on. It's small, it's not necessary, but it's about thinking, "Is there something I can do to make this easier on the other person that won't cost me anything?" Maybe you don't have time to do this, but the idea stands that when you can easily make someone's life better for them, it's a good thing to do.

Somewhat conversely, I recommend assuming the best in written communications until proven otherwise. Some people are just not great at taking advantage of the English language to convey their meaning in the polite way they intended. This is doubly true if English isn't their first language.

I once worked closely with a content marketer who wrote the nastiest internal emails. I never did understand how someone who was paid to write and presumably had a very clear understanding of the power of language could be so rude over email. Trying to listen to my own advice, I could say maybe this wasn't about me—which begged the question, what *was* it about? Or, being frank, maybe it *was* about me! Maybe she didn't like me all that much. And if I was honest, on a personal level, I didn't really like her. It's hard to hide that sort of emotion completely, no matter how professional you are.

What did I do? There's no happy ending here—but maybe a lesson. First, I went to peers I trusted who worked with her as well, wanting to understand if they also felt this way about her email tone. Maybe I was being overly sensitive. Then, I spoke to my manager about it, casually and without blaming or implying it was an issue. I just wanted to feel out if he noticed that sometimes, her emails seemed a bit curt.

Yes, he did. But he didn't think the tone was really an issue. In retrospect, I think he was lacking a real moment for empathetic leadership there. Her emails *were* curt. And it doesn't help you in the office if some people find your communication abrasive. A good manager would ideally find a way to push this woman to change her style of writing—or at least give her the opportunity to think about it.

The last common written communication area I want to look at is document commenting and ticket writing, or contributing to a shared working board, such as on Trello. These tools are a critical part of asynchronous, remote working; it's crucial to be able to work off the same document.

However, it's also often an opportunity to be the biggest jerk. I am shocked at how often document comments are passive-aggressive, rude, or denigrating. And considering there are often many people looking at a document, it's interesting how many people are willing to publicly be that way.

I like to start by giving the benefit of the doubt to the creator of any document I'm looking at and possibly commenting on. It's always easy to see a different way you would have mapped out the flow or storytelling, but that doesn't mean your way is correct. Generally, a quick once-over of the whole document before commenting does wonders.

Other ways to help you be the best contributor in a document come from asking yourself these questions:

- *What's your relationship to the creator?* Depending on your seniority, it might be okay that your comments are more top-level or based on the impressions conveyed by the slides. That's what management is paid for, to make sure the message lands well.

- *Where in the process is the creator?* An early draft may not be the time for copious grammar or small formatting comments.

- *How useful is the comment?* Will it make the document materially better? (This factor is very much related to your relationship to the creator of the document.)

- *Who's going to see this comment?* Frankly, in a distributed workforce, assume everyone will see it, and let that be your guide for what to write.

- *Might your question be answered in later sections?* The way you handle this question comes back to giving the document's creator the benefit of the doubt, not assuming they are missing some big idea you think is critical until you are sure they've left it out.

Calls/Video Calls

We've gone over the drawbacks of videoconferences, but they also are incredibly useful. Seeing people's faces makes them more real. Seeing their homes, their dogs barging in, how often the Amazon delivery person rings their doorbell—all of these are what make colleagues human. Not to mention, I've iterated many instances where voice plays a critical role in conveying what you need to express. So, when do you use phone or video calls over email or Slack? Consider these situations or purposes for a call versus written communication:

- *Time sensitivity.* If you need an answer right now, it's better to get someone on a synchronous communication channel.

- *Opportunities to humanize.* When the task is delicate, seeing someone's face and/or hearing their voice helps you modulate your delivery.

- *Ways to speed up a process.* Often on a bigger project, it's easiest to get everyone on the same channel so that nothing is lost in translation and a consensus can be reached immediately—with (hopefully) everyone having the same information.

- *Illegal things.* Just kidding. Don't do this!

- *Rude things.* Don't write down your gossip—a lesson from high school burn books that frequently needs to be relearned! And while I'm not outright suggesting you gossip over a call, it's inevitable there will be things you want to say in an office that you would never want written down.

- *Criticism.* While you can definitely give feedback over email, items that are more personal, sensitive, or heavy should be delivered as close to "in person" as possible.

- *Things people will stew over.* When you send written commentary, the recipient can parse it for nuance ad nauseam. For critical feedback, things that might happen but aren't confirmed, and hearsay, there might be negative repercussions from a format that allows for focusing so concretely on the author's word choices.

The next big question is: Do you need to use video? The answer depends. On one hand, video is our best proxy for in-person meetings. It gives a sense of presentation, can be more formal, and is the expected platform for large meetings, such as all-hands. As I've covered, video may not always be more effective than an audio call, however. I think a lot depends on how much "presenteeism" you need to convey. If you never do video calls, the team may have a sense of being checked out; but if you always do them, you're probably wasting mental energy.

Performance reviews, sensitive one-on-ones, and times when you really want to show sympathy are great for seeing someone's face. Using video implies you are giving the conversation more effort, even if, scientifically speaking, that's not true.

For all other meetings, it's worth testing out video or alternating and seeing what works best for your team. Ultimately, the medium you choose is all about making your team and colleagues feel as if they are getting the most out of their communication tools. You can survey your team and get feedback on what's working. And these norms may change over time, as the team matures or new recruits enter.

Presentations

Presentations involve the written and the verbal, combined. There's something about videoconference presentations that demands more polish. Perhaps the idea of being on-screen makes you think of television presenters. Perhaps it's the fact that you can't easily read the reactions of those listening to you. Maybe it's the ever-present threat of a dog or child banging into your workspace. Or it could be the possibility of a recording living on for eternity. Whatever the reasons, presenting on videoconference demands a more polished and practiced response.

The benefits of using video presentation include the following:

- You can more easily reference your notes.

- You can record and critique yourself later (not for the faint of heart!).

- You can alternate between showing slides and not showing them, to change the pace.

The drawbacks include

- Your gestures run the risk of distracting from your slides.

- You receive less audio feedback from the group than if you were in person. Requesting people to unmute by default helps with this issue, letting you hear chuckles or murmurs of assent.

- You don't know how much of people's attention you have if you can't see whether they are looking at you or just checking their email.

- Distracted attendees often minimize the window, so you have very little real estate, if any, beyond your voice.

- Laptops are a particularly difficult tool to work with for a variety of reasons, but having two screens can help with where to look, camera angles, note taking, and posture. Use one screen to hold the video (the one with the camera, so that you are "looking" at your audience) and the other to check your presentation.

The key to any presentation is, of course, to prep well! A well-planned presentation keeps a meeting upbeat and going strong. It's respectful of everyone to use this time to convey the necessary message as effectively as possible.

I once watched a direct report make a pitch to me and my manager for another headcount to grow her team. She and I had discussed the plan thoroughly, and I knew her argument was very persuasive, but her demeanor on the videoconference was fantastic. She had a printout of her PowerPoint in front of her so that she could maintain eye contact and pause effectively to get her points across. She'd prepared well, and the presentation was smooth. Obviously, this was an internal meeting, and the goal was not to have the slickness of a TED Talk, but it still showed the effort she'd put into her thoughts and how she wanted to walk us through them.

Creative Communication

Humanity and fun can be lacking from a virtual workplace, turning any organization into more of an output factory than a coalition of people trying to achieve things. Verbal communication is richly nuanced in a way that most writing can never be. You must take advantage of what you have though, which is GIFs, emojis, and the fantastic site *https://conventionalcomments. org/*, which helps you reword comments to be more actionable and less personal. With sarcasm and jokes in general, using rich communication options can help you make sure your humor is understood.

As we've discussed, empathetic communication is about thinking through how you convey what you want to say so that the other person can hear it or read the message in the most effective way possible. It's about putting their perspective first as you craft your communication.

One key element of this empathetic approach to communication is remembering that others may not always understand your tone. Some people are fantastic at conveying tone with the written word, but this is definitely not everyone's greatest skill, and that's okay! Likewise, some people aren't great at picking up tone, jokes, or other more nuanced sentiments. You want to make it easy on people to understand your meaning, and the way you craft your message plays a role.

I wanted to write a whole chapter on GIFs and emojis. I think they might be among the most undervalued communication tools in our modern arsenal. People complain that it's hard to convey tone over email and Slack. Not if you use a purpose-built emoji! I get a lot of flak for my excessive use of cheesy GIFs, but at least my colleagues know there's a human on the other end of the line—one who's trying to convey emotions. Having had totally remote managers as well as direct reports, I have found it valuable to sprinkle our conversations with emotions. This is the thread of conversation, the extra information that body language conveys. Emojis play the same role, adding one more layer of meaning that humans crave to help translate interpersonal communications. Sarcasm, jokes, laughter—all of these are easier to convey with images, as opposed to text.

Also, even if people don't exactly get your joke, the insertion of a GIF or emoji at least makes it clear that you are trying to make a joke. And trying is half the battle!

Beware, though, of passive-aggressive emojis. If your email isn't funny or particularly nice, because the topic is more formal or demanding of a more serious tone, don't try to lighten it up with an emoji. Using one just rings false and doesn't endear you to your recipients. Quite the opposite, your recipients may perceive this as passive aggression and be more affected by that than by the message of the email. There are also generational differences in perception of emojis. Because of shifting norms, it's usually better to stick with the tried-and-true (like basic smiley or frowning faces) if you don't know your audience well.

Cross-Cultural Communication

Sometimes, an understanding of someone's perspective is really hampered by cultural differences, and this is ever more true in a remote-first, global culture. The biggest hurdles I've seen fall into these categories:

- Stereotypes of communication styles

- English as a second language

- Time zone challenges

I have worked primarily in global roles, managing and being managed, influencing and partnering across time zones and cultural norms. A lot of people have heard the usual generalizations about cultural norms. And we all know that stereotyping has many negative ramifications. Working in this setting also, however, allows us to quickly categorize other people's behaviors and know that *it's not about us; it's about them.* Some cultures are known for giving critical feedback swiftly and without tempering it to seem "nicer." But of course, not everyone from that culture is going to give you harsh feedback to your face. There's always room for nuance. For me, as an American, when I've worked with people who were very quick to give direct feedback in a way that felt culturally differerent, it was a bit of a trial by fire in terms of seeing feedback and *"radical candor"* (from Kim Scott's book, "the ability to challenge directly" and "show that you care personally" at the same time[12]) in action.

Often, teams with a lot of international experience are more able to recognize their cultural differences and how they are perceived, letting colleagues from other cultures know they might be in for a bit of shock. In other words, if you can name it, you can control it. Being transparent about your communication styles, your abilities, and drawbacks is a good first step. Everyone likes to know who they are working with. It's a great topic to include in any icebreakers or opening conversations in a cross-cultural team—asking questions such as "What's the one stereotype about your culture you embody, and what's the one you don't?" It's both illustrative of what stereotypes exist out there and how your teammates do and don't fit those molds.

There's no silver bullet for cross-cultural stereotypes because there are so many diverging subgroups, ages, gender identities, and upbringings. The starting point for empathy and unraveling stereotypes when working cross-culturally is, of course, to go in with an open mind, acknowedging that people and cultures are different and that these differences will affect your work styles. Transparency—as well as an open acknowledgement of trying to do the best you can within the limitations of what you have known up until this point—goes a long way.

Understanding how naturally empathetic the members of your team are is also useful, not to mention something you should try to hire for. Being able to consider other people's perspectives is critical in working in a global environment. A French study looked at people's ability to adjust to an expatriate work assignment and saw a correlation between their emotional intelligence and ability to thrive in a novel environment.[13]

English is not everyone's first language. The more native English speakers repeat this truth and try to remember that non-native speakers are doing their job in a second language every day, the easier it can be for them to forgive errors, not assume slights or insults, and help others to convey their thoughts without being condescending. This is another area where the Conventional Comments website can be helpful, because it helps you display empathy in correcting someone's work. You should try to make the message as nonpersonal and as helpful or action-oriented as possible. And if you need filler words or softeners to do that, using them is better for everyone.

Lastly, time zones can play a role in cross-cultural work. This idea is basic yet often ignored. Different cultures have different workplace time norms. And everyone has personal lives they need to attend to. Working with your team to be explicit about what is a possibility, what is optimal, and what times are absolutely untouchable as personal time is a key exercise when working across time zones. Making this effort is about respecting others' time and acknowledging their needs, while being open about the needs of the business—digital empathy across the clock!

Delivering your messages in a virtual world takes a new approach, one that has to be reflected on and then mastered, since the switch to a digital-first workforce happened almost overnight for many. Using your body language, your physical space, and your mediums to convey your messages effectively to those around you will pay professional dividends, not just in remote work, but as some transition to hybrid or even back to the old-fashioned office.

SECTION 2

MANAGING A VIRTUAL TEAM USING DIGITAL EMPATHY

CHAPTER 4

DRIVING REAL CONNECTION WITH YOUR TEAM

HOW DO YOU TRANSLATE being a great manager mostly in person to being a great manager mostly at a distance? The techniques for building teams, finding connection, and inspiring your teams have to change to meet the new media we use to communicate. In this chapter, you'll find ways to build true rapport online, maximize your communications for effectiveness, and inspire success among your team members using the tools available to you. Having happy team members who feel safe, inspired, and clear about their work is the same both offline and online; the actions required to get there, however, need tweaking for this new world. This is *How to Lead Online 101*.

Why Focus on Connection Within Your Team?

As we discussed in earlier chapters, working from home takes away a lot of the natural methods by which people build rapport in the office. Not to mention, many teams are not able to achieve these traits even in in-person situations. Yet doing so is crucial. A wealth of research explores the relationship between team cohesiveness and success. While different studies call it *engagement, emotional intelligence,* or having *productive norms,* all of these concepts require that both management and the team act empathetically—able to consider others' perspectives.

The survey company Gallup has researched a lot of ways that teams succeed or not, and found engagement is a significant driver. *Gallup defines engaged employees as those who are involved in, enthusiastic about, and committed to their work and workplace.* Work units in the top quartile of engagement see 17 percent higher productivity, 20 percent higher sales, and 21 percent higher profitability than those in the bottom quartile. Enjoying your time with your colleagues, as well as trusting them, can be critical to this engagement. An even more interesting finding from Gallup polls is a "concrete link between having a best friend at work and the amount of effort employees expend in their job. Particularly for women, those who strongly agree they have a best friend at work are more than twice as likely to be engaged (63 percent) compared with the women who say otherwise (29 percent)."[1]

The takeaway is that your emotional investment in those around you, colleagues and teammates, plays a huge role in how an organization thrives. What is a best friend if not someone whose feelings you care about? Going into work each day and genuinely caring about those around you, even if it applies to some more than others, is a natural extension of empathy. You want the best for them, you want to mitigate bad things that happen to them, and you feel tied to the way they perceive the things that happen.

Many other studies have defined the predictive qualities of a strong team as *good communication,* which includes ensuring that every member is given a chance to speak; and *social sensitivity,* which refers to members' ability to understand each other's thoughts and feelings and respectfully engage in disagreements. I think we could pretty much summarize those ideas as *empathy.* Getting along well, building community, and perspective taking are somewhat inherent in an office, where unspoken norms are relatively easily transmitted. But when you move to a distributed team, everything changes.

How to Drive Real Connection with Your Team

The success of any team is rooted in its abilities to achieve its goals. People who are happier and feel safer in their work environment are better able to achieve their goals. Creating this team atmosphere is perhaps the single most important thing a leader can do to drive achievement from and with their team. I've mentioned Google's Project Aristotle and its emphasis on the trait successful teams share, which is a culture of *psychological safety*. If you want to create a culture of psychological safety on your team, or of other traits that you think will help your team function better as a cohesive whole, it's critical to think about this carefully and be thoughtful and demanding in your implementation.

To think about connection within a team, we start at the top, looking at *culture*, and then get more granular, with team and one-on-one relationship building. Combined, these factors contribute to an effective team environment, virtually and in person.

Culture in a Virtual Team

Culture is the foundation for an environment that allows people to be successful. When people understand their work environment, its norms, and what to expect, they are free to do their best work. A positive and growth-oriented culture is ideal for a team to thrive.

When I think about one of the biggest challenges brought on by working remotely, a huge stumbling block is conveying company culture. Why?

1. Most people find it hard to define "culture."

2. Most companies, while they may have explicit values, haven't thought about how these values trickle down to culture.

3. Culture has all too often been used as an exclusionary social tool to make people of different backgrounds or beliefs feel out of sync with their peers. This, rightly, makes people fearful about being too prescriptive with culture.

Tack on the pains of being physically distant from your colleagues, and you have a perfect storm.

Step 1: So What Is Your Culture?

Culture is the values, norms, and behaviors that define how you do business. Some pieces of information you might pick up explicitly or implicitly about a team's culture are

- What projects have been delivered and at what speed? What was valued (e.g., speed over perfection or vice versa)?

- What happens when you fail? Is that information embarrassing or a tool for learning?

- What are the hours people work (is it okay to go for a run in the middle of the day, etc.)?

- What are the cadence and style of communication? How often do people check in with each other? How acceptable is swearing?

In every organization, the answers to these and other similar culture-defining questions are evocative and contribute to the de facto definition of a company's culture. In a "normal" office environment, you'd see these behaviors happening and learn from them. But in a virtual setting, so many are invisible to anyone not directly involved.

It's worth asking relative newcomers as well as "old hands" to define the team's culture, particularly from a virtual perspective, to understand where you might need to explicitly outline people's expectations in their new work-life. Like so many things in a virtual office, your culture needs to be more clearly defined and communicated. Then write out a manifesto or playbook for it, spelling it out to make your culture clear to your people.

Step 2: How Do Values Turn into Culture?

Value statements are usually a collection of hopeful but sometimes vague beliefs and philosophies designed to be a north star for the company. They are something you can hold actions up to and say, "Does this *feel* right?" But this is not the same as *culture*. Culture refers to the everyday actions that stem from this guiding set of principles.

Values can turn into culture by hard work, luck, or not at all. After working within your team and organization, can you identify what cultural norms exist in your company? The next necessary question is to ask whether these values align with the stated values and mission of the company.

If your company's mission is, say, to move fast and break things, but your team functions in a way that values perfection over speed and saving face over learning from mistakes, your culture and values are mismatched. This is confusing for all employees, but especially newcomers, who may not be able to deal with the disconnect. **Map the culture from Step 1 to the values and make sure there are no disconnects. Then, codify this information in onboarding meetings, playbooks, and/or the company handbook.** In a distributed workforce, documentation is key!

Don't Let Culture Be a Weapon

We can't ignore how culture can also make people feel excluded. Just one example: think of a traditional investment banking culture, with very late hours and a value on presenteeism. How does this culture work for parents, both men and women? No one wants to live in that world anymore.

After you've mapped out what your culture is and how it aligns with your values, the last step is to make sure this doesn't leave anyone out. **Ask yourself, in conjunction with a group of people representing different perspectives, "What about this might not work for some people?"** You can't please everyone, but you have to be certain ignorance doesn't cause you to exclude valuable team members.

The massive overhaul of working norms that came with the pandemic presented a perfect time to implement changes that welcomed diversity. If your culture transcends virtual and breeds happiness and success, you've nailed it.

Why Do We Bother with Team Building?

What is team building? If culture is the passive term, team building is the active part. It's the efforts of leadership to strengthen the bonds between coworkers, individually and as a group, to set a sense of communal purpose and camaraderie that separates one working group from another. This is deeply related to the idea of humanizing the workplace.

From *Understanding Management*, by Richard Daft and Dorothy Marcic, "Morale is also higher in cohesive teams because of increased team member communication, friendly team environment, loyalty, and team member contribution in the decision-making process."[2]

It's sometimes easier to picture in the negative: if the situation gets really bad on your team, with a total lack of cohesion, people start building up their threat response. According to David Rock, the director of the NeuroLeadership Institute, "The threat response is both mentally taxing and deadly to the productivity of a person. . . . Because this response uses up oxygen and glucose from the blood, they are diverted from other parts of the brain—including the working memory function, which processes new information and ideas. This impairs analytic thinking, creative insight, and problem solving."[3] In other words, just when people most need their sophisticated mental capabilities, the brain's internal resources are taken away from them. This really hammers home how a bad working environment can actually make your team less smart!

For me, the entire theory behind team building is that it's much easier to put yourself in another person's shoes when you've created a relationship with them. The ideal is to create a culture of psychological safety, starting with a culture where you aren't afraid to fail or voice dissent. But a true culture of safety is more comprehensive. It's about bringing your whole, authentic self to work.

The business case behind this is clear: happier people stay at companies longer. And retention is everything. Having a team that stays for longer periods of time—not to say forever but enough to become a well-oiled machine and not to waste excessive time recruiting and training—is worth its weight in gold.

In a remote workspace, this strengthening of bonds between people is inherently more difficult. But this is where the fun comes in! Once you have some thoughts and goals for how your culture should work, it's time to have some fun putting that culture into place. You want your team to feel as though they can bring their whole selves to work. They can try things out and fail, and they can embarrass themselves lightly without bringing ridicule in a culture of psychological safety.

If you don't have a safe space as a team to allow for imperfection and innovation, no team-building activities will get off the ground because people will be too busy trying to protect themselves. Studies have shown that people who don't deem a social situation as safe adopt behaviors to protect themselves, such as talking only briefly and not talking about themselves, basically backing away from any opportunity for bonding.

So how do you build these connections? So many activities for building rapport have, in the past, stemmed from getting the team out drinking beers. For many reasons, this approach doesn't work for everyone. Even pre-pandemic, the idea that people would go out drinking after work, taking away time from their family or other obligations, was losing steam. One of my English managers would tease me that my team outings were the cheapest ever expensed. A number of people on my team didn't drink, and we all voted for outings that didn't involve alcohol, although abstaining wasn't really the custom in the pub-loving UK.

You also want activities or options for people who are both introverts and extroverts. How do you make small talk easy for people who loathe small talk? You don't need alcohol to get to know people. You need situations that get people out of their comfort zone a tiny bit. This is why competition works so well.

And if the coronavirus pandemic taught us anything, alcohol consumed alone over videoconference isn't really the same kind of fun for camaraderie building anyway.

Practical Implementation of Virtual Team Building

For your team bonding, there are several key aspects to keep in mind: *goal, timing,* and *delight.* Each aspect has spectrums within to consider when mapping out an ideal set of team-building activities. Anything that gives your team an "other" to discuss and coalesce around is great for building rapport among different personalities. This is why competitive team-building projects like escape rooms or baking competitions can drive team coalescence. But be careful of asking people to share too much.

Goal

I said the ultimate goal of team building is psychological safety. But each event should have more concrete goals as well. What are you hoping to get out of this event? The three spectrums I think of for goals in this context are

1. **Social versus Business Skill Building:** Technical skill acquisition to improve output versus opportunities to create social bonds

2. **Personally Revealing versus Superficial:** How emotional or intimate is the activity?

3. **Collaborative versus Competitive:** Traditional bonding idea of creating an "other" for a team to rally against

The far ends of each spectrum—that is, events with absolutely zero learning potential versus events that are purely for learning—have their uses, and a great team-building calendar would touch on points all along each spectrum throughout the year to create the right attitudes, motivations, and excitement around the team-building strategy.

Social versus Business Skill Building

The first spectrum of team-building activities we look at involves those that operate from purely *business goals* (such as brainstorming features of a new product) to a purely *social goal* (such as a cocktail-making course). Not to say social goals don't have business implications; for the purpose of structuring different opportunities, we call them *social* and *skill building*.

Unstructured time for people to just chat can be great for deepening bonds that are already there, but most people getting after-work drinks tend to gravitate toward people they already know. Mixing up these fun activities with "forced fun" is a great way for people to casually interact with and enjoy their colleagues in a nonwork context. This is also a great time to introduce creativity, getting people outside of their comfort zones.

As much as random, virtual "coffee chats" can seem like a waste of time, they are critical for building the bonds that allow you to function as one team, even if you're actually from different teams. When you start a team project, in addition to the basic icebreaker, it's nice to create a document with everyone's bios and a little insight into them, whatever they want to share. This document becomes something people can reflect back on and reference when they need to understand exactly which team Thomas from Finance reports into.

Four key factors make these social icebreakers or team-building activities work:

- *Your activity can't be too intentionally revealing.* For example, making a vision board for your best self is something you do among friends, but some people may find that incredibly invasive among colleagues.

- *The activity must work for people who have less creative talent.* It's not fun for people to compete at something they have no chance of winning based on skills they already hold. For example, you can allow people to succeed in multiple ways—from using words to drawing and singing to harnessing teamwork. Not everyone wants to join an individual limerick or painting contest! I've seen group art classes where the supplies are sent home to everyone, a teacher is Zoomed in, and everyone gets a chance to flex a muscle they may not use too often. But there's no winning; in fact, you don't even have to share your creation.

- *Ideally, the activity should not take up too much personal time.* This point should be self-evident, but not everyone's evenings are free for socializing. Consider the different segments of your team, culture, age, and family situations to decide what might land well across the group.

- *Consider the size of the group.* Videoconferencing has some limitations due to the time lags and unnatural cadence of speaking. Smaller is better for virtual meetings. A roundtable of six is good for sharing, eight is pushing it, and anything beyond that is nuts.

Conversely, bonding through business skill building is the easiest to quantify and budget for. Public speaking is a classic example, but of course, there are many "courses" you can take and offer. Skill building also offers the opportunity for asynchronous learning, to take a course at your own leisure and then sync up on the results.

A good manager creates not only opportunities for skills directly related to the teams' work—such as an advanced Excel course for junior finance colleagues—but also opportunities for general professional development. Everyone benefits from learning better public speaking and better strategic thinking, or giving better feedback.

One event not found in these categories is *celebrating the team's success*. This type of event offers a key moment in team building, as there is a natural coalescence around a shared achievement that can be celebrated and should naturally be included in a group moment of celebration.

Personally Revealing versus Superficial

How much will people share? Some team-building events, such as life mapping, are extremely intimate. And some are not, such as a pottery-making course. What is the right balance?

For some people, a public-speaking course is extremely intimate. Anything that is frightening has the opportunity to be (too) revealing for people. But it also is great at breaking down boundaries. Anything that could be frightening is revealing and vice versa, and thus should be used carefully if the team isn't already in a comfortable place of safety and intimacy, where putting themselves in a vulnerable position won't lead to someone breaking down and leaving in tears. Trust is gained in personally revealing activities, but the effectiveness depends on the team's state going into the event. There are also benefits and drawbacks to at-home and in-person participation in these intimate activities. Some people might feel safer doing these things from home, without having to be face to face with colleagues. For some, that feeling of distance may exacerbate their discomfort with revealing so much about themselves.

Any team building that allows people to get to know each other personally is also helpful in breaking down a tendency toward parochial empathy.

Studies have shown that you can reduce the negative stereotypes you attribute to people who are different from you by learning facts about them as individuals, in order to see them on their own, not as part of an "other." Even completely irrelevant information, such as how someone takes their coffee or tea, can work against negative stereotypes you may hold against that person's group.[4] In the "olden" days, that is, before the pandemic, this was easier to solve because offices and after-work socializing provided opportunities to get out of the work relationship frame and learn more about individuals. Because getting to know each other is harder to do naturally over Zoom, intentionally getting to know your colleagues as people is even more imperative.

There's also another option for revealing team building: activities that are professionally revealing, where teammates get to know each other's strengths, work styles, or past successes. Activities like personality mapping, such as Myers–Briggs assessments, fit into this category.

Collaborative versus Competitive

Some wonderful, classic team activities are both competitive and collaborative, such as paintball, multiplayer videogames, softball—anything where the whole team functions *as a team* to achieve a goal. Some activities are more solo competitive, like throwing darts or Peloton mileage competitions. And some are completely collaborative, like the whole team participating in an escape room. What type of team bonding are you trying to foster? General, collaborative activities can be useful in everyday scenarios, while inspiring an "us versus them" mentality can be more useful when facing a novel, significant challenge.

One notion to consider when planning collaborative versus competitive team building is the idea of *parochial empathy*—people are more empathetic to those in their "tribe," depending on how you define that tribe. Paul Bloom's book *Against Empathy: The Case for Rational Compassion* makes the argument against empathy for this reason.[5] Instinctively, empathy is toward your tribe, in this case, your immediate team. You can both harness and diminish this bias, depending on who is in which group and what type of competition you get involved in. If you are working on a complex project with people who generally don't work together, putting them in a situation where they have to bond with some people as part of a team against others is a good harnessing of parochial empathy; you want the team to feel united in their task.

Timing: Annual versus Daily

You will want to find the right rhythm for team events. Too few, and you risk disenchanting your team as well as overhyping the few events you do have. Too many, and the returns diminish, as people feel you are wasting their time. The cadence is also affected by the types of events. It's easy to see how too many technical, daylong training programs would overwhelm the team. Having a team of chair masseuses come in every day at 5:00 p.m. might be less demanding. Ahem.

Ask yourself: "How often does this need to happen, how much can I afford, and what is an acceptable demand on people's time?" Taking time to team build is a requirement for successful teams, not a distraction from real work. But no one on the team gets their annual bonus for being really great at a paintball offsite, so these time demands have to be balanced.

Coordinated versus Asynchronous

Particularly in a hybrid workforce, finding ways to drive rapport, camaraderie, and connection in an asynchronous way will be paramount. People bringing their whole selves to work in a way that persists is complicated. For example, this is why Snapchat was so successful. People were much more willing to share personal information if their video died in twenty-four hours. Thus, asynchronous isn't great for emotional and socially complicated team-building events, but it can be good for lighthearted, more frequent sharing—like a bake club or TV show review on Slack.

Consider the following examples.

ASYNCHRONOUS TEAM BUILDING Have every person on the team list a strength about every other person on the team anonymously; then, distribute the lists to the recipients. Some people will keep these lists for years as a reminder of all the positive things people see in them. You could also do this as a Secret Santa–type game, where you have to give someone a nice, thoughtful piece of feedback, after drawing their name from a hat. And if you don't know them well, you'll have to solicit that information from others, so it's doubly rewarding.

- Recipe club. Everyone works off the same recipe or concept, say chocolate chip cookies, and shares their successes or failings. Bonus points for mailing examples to your colleagues.

- Visual bake sale. The team bakes something off one recipe, in an effort to come up with the most visually appealing baked goods. Points also awarded for the biggest failures!

- Book club/movie club/podcast club. Everyone can approach the same entertainment, at the same pace; no binging allowed! Live Slack chats can add a synchronous element, but gathering one-on-one to discuss is a way to make it less time bound.

HYBRID TEAM BUILDING Consider the following:

- Meyers-Briggs–type training/life mapping. This could be anything where a large part is taking the survey, and the output is important and not skill based.

- Bingo. It is competitive and gives people something to talk about.

VIRTUAL SYNCHRONOUS TEAM BUILDING Consider the following:

- Escape rooms. Make sure they highlight either a competition or a chance to collaborate. If everyone is solving the same puzzle alone, it doesn't give you much.

- Magician performance over videoconference or digital travel experience (e.g., the type offered by Airbnb where you can "tour" a city)

- Your own scavenger hunt or office bingo

- Childlike wonder—ice cream sundaes delivered, painting/art class

- The Donut app in Slack, which sets up random colleagues to casually chat

- Sharing of funny videos and cat memes

- Online games! For example, bingo.

For hybrid teams, it's even more critical to weigh which events need to be in person and how often they need to happen, with some team bonding still happening online.

Delight: Simple versus Designed to Delight

Delight is a way of saying an activity is a special treat, such as getting a famous cocktail maker over video to teach you how to use craft ingredients that are sent to everyone's house ahead of time versus everyone grabbing a glass of their favorite beverage and doing a basic happy hour. This idea has obviously been advanced by the large tech companies, which, in an effort to retain happy workers, have created delightful work environments with beer on tap and candy-stocked kitchens, among other perks. Employees like to be treated nicely. These perks aren't substitutes for fair pay, flexible leave policies, and so on, that also delight employees, but treating your employees to something delightful every once in a while is great for happiness and morale.

One-on-One Management Connections

While fostering a great team environment is critical for you as a leader, you also want to have strong bonds with each of your direct reports.

Bring your whole self to work; the only way to make sure your connections with your team are honest and true is to start with yourself. Being open about who you are, acknowledging (to the best of your abilities) your flaws and opportunities to improve, and letting people into your personal life at least a little are critical for opening the door to true connections with your teams. Not everyone at work will end up best friends, but if you allow your true self to shine through, you can always find facets to connect with that will be richer than just the transactional work information you must convey.

Schedule your one-on-ones to accommodate *your team members'* needs; different people need different one-on-one frequencies, lengths, and structures. You want your direct reports to use your time in the most effective way, so it's worth mapping out what the goals of one-on-ones are. Then determine if they are arranged to best meet those goals.

Especially in a remote situation, you need to recalibrate to make sure you are giving people the attention they would have ordinarily gotten from just sitting near you in the office. Sometimes, it's helpful to have one-off meetings after larger meetings or events, as a rolling meeting to re-create that casual debrief when walking out of a large, all-hands, or other more top-level meeting. As people mature and roles change, these structures will change, too, so it's good to remember nothing is ever set in stone.

An underemphasized management technique is looking for opportunities for your team members to get off your team. Counterintuitive but true! While retention is hugely valuable, people don't usually stay on one team forever, particularly if there are no opportunities for promotion. With all of the digital learning opportunities available, and especially with some free time being created with the reduction in commutes and wasted office time, there's an opportunity to upskill your team. And if you take your team members' eventual departures seriously, you are more likely to get long notice periods and help finding replacements than if they leave because they don't feel management cares about their promotions.

Praise

We cover this issue more fully in Chapter 5, "Giving Feedback Online," especially as it pertains to virtual settings, but studies have shown that manager appreciation is one of the critical indicators, if not *the* critical indicator, that an employee will thrive in their role. Be direct, specific, and as frequent as possible with your praise.

Constantly nudge others toward being their best selves. You want your team to get better under your tutelage—to move forward in their roles and their careers. Constantly holding them to a higher standard, letting them know how to improve, helps them level up.

Creating a culture your team can thrive in is one of the (not the most) important things you can do as a manager. But it almost never happens accidentally. By being thoughtful about what culture should look like from a values perspective to how it actually manifests day to day, managers create a foundation for their employees to get their work done on an interpersonal level. And the successful bonding between teams and employees creates the necessary level of engagement to drive success, both as humans and as corporations.

CHAPTER 5
GIVING FEEDBACK ONLINE

ONE OF YOUR MOST important actions as a manager is to give your team effective feedback. But in a digital world, we've lost three major aspects to giving feedback:

- *Synchronicity.* People won't always receive feedback in real time, without the line of sight available in a physical setting.

- *Spontaneity.* It's much harder to grab someone casually after a virtual presentation to follow up and discuss more details. You will need to get their attention first, by scheduling a meeting or pinging them on Slack.

- *Intimacy.* More of our communications in a digital setting become written, rather than spoken face to face; thus, our intimacy changes.

So how do these changes affect the art of giving feedback, including criticism? This chapter covers:

- Why do we give feedback, and how does this help build management rapport?

- What's my motivation?

- Who is receiving the message, and what is their state of mind?

- How and when will I deliver this feedback?

This new remote world requires even more consideration of how to provide feedback, including criticism, than its in-person counterpart. Giving feedback is a key moment when what you think, say, and do won't necessarily be perceived by the recipient in the same way, sometimes with very painful repercussions. Virtual feedback erases a lot of our empathetic tools to ensure the recipient hears the feedback in a useful/constructive way. These changes can be more consequential for criticism than praise, but both are critical tools in a manager's toolbox.

Why Do We Give Feedback, and How Does This Help Build Management Rapport?

The arguments for providing positive feedback are many, and we cover those in the "Praise or Positive Feedback" section of this chapter. But in applying critical feedback, managers often get stuck. Giving critical feedback involves three components that are critical to building an engaged team:

- Respect
- Opportunity
- The team's success

If you truly respect your direct reports, you want to apply the golden rule: Treat them as you wish to be treated. This means giving hard feedback to contribute to their success.

Criticism can be a major opportunity to improve. If you don't give actionable, useful criticism to those around you, how are they supposed to know how to grow? You are giving them the gift of opportunity. Frankly, not giving necessary critical feedback is a cruel type of management.

Besides an individual's growth being dependent on feedback, the team's success rides on achieving the stated goals. If someone's output needs to change to meet that objective, then of course, they must be coached into changing that behavior. Also, the whole team needs to see that you manage by respecting people enough to help them improve and achieve goals. The community understanding of this respect and opportunity is critical in defining yourself as a manager who values your team's growth.

Providing (or receiving) this feedback is not comfortable, and it's often not easy, especially at first. If you can't bring yourself to be uncomfortable— even though, through that discomfort, you are allowing them an opportunity to be more successful—it's a sign of disrespect. The only way to really show you care about people is to help them be their best selves, and sometimes, that means sharing hard truths. So how do you do it?

What's My Motivation?

Any discussion of giving critical feedback needs to start with analyzing your motivation. Without understanding why you want to convey this feedback, deciding how and when to give it is hard.

SO, WHY *ARE* YOU GIVING THIS FEEDBACK? Feedback is inherently biased. We can't get around that, but it's important to remember the objective: *to make the other person better!* Giving criticism makes people better. It's empirical. Thus, it is a kindness, even if it hurts in the short term. Studies indicate that feedback recipients who get unfavorable ratings tend to improve their performance more than those who get better ratings.[1]

The answer to this question—*what's my motivation?*—really must be that you believe the recipient can take this feedback, act on it, and improve.

AS YOU PREPARE TO GIVE FEEDBACK, AND WHILE GIVING IT, ASK YOURSELF, "IS WHAT I'M TELLING THIS PERSON ACTIONABLE?" Vague feedback is almost useless. If you can't make clear what needs to be addressed, then the feedback is more about how whatever you are discussing made you, the the giver, *feel,* rather than a business impact. I'm not saying that your feelings may not be a business impact in and of themselves, but your feelings don't make for very useful feedback. Feedback should be specific, actionable, and *helpful.*

Use behavioral terms as much as possible when describing what you'd like someone to do differently. Instead of saying, "You have a bad attitude," let them know exactly what constitutes this bad attitude, like "I noticed you rolled your eyes and sighed on Zoom when Jenny spoke about the new product line." Then, talk about what you would like to see instead. One option is, "While I know you're passionate about this topic, I'd like to ask you to contribute constructive questions if you have a concern. This approach lets your colleagues understand your concerns without becoming defensive."

Even if it's hard to hear, getting feedback is the only way to learn.

ANOTHER QUESTION TO ASK YOURSELF IS: "AM I THE RIGHT PERSON TO GIVE THIS FEEDBACK?" If you need someone else's opinion to ensure your critique carries the right weight, why are you the one giving it? (The opposite of this is, of course, praise. If it's warranted, sharing how other people thought something was great is always appreciated.)

Understanding how other people in your organization perceive an issue can be helpful in structuring your critique to make sure it's actionable. As an example, my manager and I once watched a presentation done by someone on my team. I knew this presentation wasn't the best this man could do. He lacked enthusiasm and didn't approach the presentation as the internal sales pitch it effectively was. Given his background and history of unenthusiastic presentations, I formulated some feedback about pumping up the volume. But by situational accident, my manager had a chance to speak with this man first and gave his thoughts on why the proposal didn't land. My manager was focused on the end result, that the presentation wasn't well received, and gently prodded the man for solutions on how he could do better next time. In later check-ins with my direct report, I saw that receiving my manager's feedback, in a gentle, questioning way, had really impressed upon him the need to do better. He and I could then work on practicing the skills to improve his delivery, as his motivation had increased with the attention from a higher-up.

Using another mouthpiece to deliver this message with more authority is one great example. Another is more tied to remote work, given the emotional distance that can exist between people who have never met. Some colleagues may have deeper bonds due to more time spent in person, and thus have a better foundation from which to give criticism.

WHETHER YOU ARE THE GIVER OR RECEIVER OF FEEDBACK, A HELPFUL QUESTION TO CONSIDER IS: "HOW MUCH OF THE FEEDBACK IS REALLY A REFLECTION OF THE PERSON GIVING IT?" This happens, regardless of our intentions. I like to call this feedback, "I'm talking about you, but I'm talking about me." I don't mean to discount the feedback or say that it's not correct, but it's a good question to ask yourself as you prepare to give feedback. I had a manager who loved to go through the details of PowerPoints early on in the creation of presentations. In retrospect, it must have killed him to go through my first drafts, which were riddled with formatting errors and typos. To me, those weren't worth dealing with until the value and message of the presentation had been cemented, but to him, they were very important. Because we were working in two different countries, he wasn't seeing my work process, only outputs, and the typos were driving him nuts.

What could we both have done better in this situation? In an ideal world, he could have told me, "This just really bugs me." I knew the issue was not the quality of my final output, but on a personal level, the process wasn't working for him. Could I have changed? Maybe. Some ways of working are ingrained, and I definitely prefer to get the big picture down before perfecting something. But if he was receiving my work as sloppy, even mid-process, that's something I needed to change. I read his nonverbal cues and small comments about the work correctly in the end, but probably too slowly.

So why bother? While giving feedback may not be perfect, I'm sure every reader of this book can look back on some very useful criticisms they've received in their career. Some feedback moments can positively change an entire career. Understanding that there is an innate level of bias can help both givers and receivers to take feedback opportunities with a grain of salt.

Who Is Receiving the Message, and What Is Their State of Mind?

You must consider the delicate social web surrounding you and how that might affect your delivery of feedback. You should be thinking about how deep your *real* bond is. Do you feel this is someone you've really connected with, either in person or digitally? Delivering feedback deftly without a connection can be a lot harder. It doesn't mean that you shouldn't give the feedback, but that you might want to give your motivation and medium more scrutiny, so that this feedback isn't the most defining memory of you this recipient will have.

Also, consider perceived seniority, perceived state of mind, as well as outside factors that can affect people, such as time of day. These are, of course, considerable issues, as we test out the best ways to work remotely.

Focusing on creating the right team and forging one-on-one connections to create a culture where feedback is taken positively is a key reason to spend time working on your team culture.

People who are just learning a skill—perhaps more junior people you work with—might want more positive feedback. Studies have shown that beginners tend to prefer an emphasis on what they are doing right, whereas advanced practitioners of a skill prefer critical feedback. This distinction makes intuitive sense; you don't want to knock the confidence out of someone with little skill in an area. There's room here for the dreaded *compliment sandwich*, much lambasted, where you sandwich criticism between positive feedback. How you approach this situation comes back to empathy and putting yourself in their shoes. You don't want someone's brain to be so overwhelmed by the threat response that criticism triggers them, rather than helps them get better. What you say depends on your listener: if they will be so focused on the positive feedback that they won't hear the opportunity for improvement or whether the praise will merely soften the blow.

Particularly with junior members of the term, any feedback can be taken very seriously and might last for years. Unless you are the guru of whatever skill you are critiquing, it's helpful to point out that you feel this way, but maybe not everyone will.

One way to frame your delivery is in the context of minimizing the threat response. Have they just walked out of a tense conversation, and their cortisol levels are likely to be high? Or is it 3:00 p.m. on a quiet Friday, and you're just reading through a document they sent over? Receiving negative feedback often causes people to feel threatened. This threat response is both unpleasant and, more importantly, not helpful in terms of acting upon your advice. A study from Case Western showed that people who feel threatened don't improve. Criticism "inhibits access to existing neural circuits and invokes cognitive, emotional, and perceptual impairment," the researchers found.[2]

In a virtual setting, it can be hard to know what state someone is in because you can't read any of their body language. But you can start by asking, "Hey, how are you?" and if their response is a frazzled, "I'm so busy," or something similar, it might not be the time to deliver negative feedback.

I'm not a big fan of leading with, "I'd like to give you some feedback. Would that work for you?" because it's a rhetorical question. If they aren't in the right space, they might stew until you come back to it. The polite approach is to let them know it's coming, but not under the guise of choosing the time to deliver the feedback. A consultant friend of mine tells a story I'm sure we can all commiserate with. A client once told this consultant they needed to talk, and the consultant became nervous that the client was going to take them off the project or something. The consultant became paranoid, but it turned out the client was delaying their project for technology reasons and they needed my friend to know, since they were managing their communications. The gap in time between when my friend heard "we need to talk" and when they found out why led to some white knuckling and second guessing about what they could possibly have done wrong!

Another way to think about this situation is to consider the context for your team members personally. Do they have a reason why they are underperforming, such as issues at home or health problems? Again, the context can help you to convey your feedback in a way that is useful and doesn't pile on top of the other issues affecting their work.

When you're giving serious negative feedback to someone, it's good to know if they see it coming. How to land your commentary might be affected by how likely they are to be expecting it. If, after a particularly bad presentation, where someone clearly bombed—they were uncomfortable on stage and did progressively worse as the presentation went on—you wanted to give some (specific, actionable, and *helpful)* feedback, you would likely want to couch it very carefully, taking note of the fact that they likely already know it didn't go well. It's useful to focus on what can be fixed while also being sympathetic to the feeling of failure they are likely experiencing. If the opposite is true—they appear to feel as if they "nailed" a presentation, and you think some things needed upgrading—you will want to avoid purposefully deflating their ego. The open-mindedness required to apply feedback effectively can easily be shut down by very negative language.

A study by Paul Green, Francesca Gino, and Bradley R. Staats at Harvard Business School showed that people tend to distance themselves from people who give them negative feedback. It weakens their sense of self.[3] You should try to protect that sense of self and value without sugarcoating the feedback. You do this by accompanying negative feedback with validation of who people are and the value they provide to your organization. This approach is not about providing this validation all the time, but people do sometimes need to feel valued as a foundation for any negative feedback they may receive.

Another issue to keep in mind, and perhaps keep track of, is how much feedback and of what type you are giving. You have fewer interactions with people in a virtual office, so you need to be aware of what percentage of your feedback is negative so that it doesn't seem as if all your interactions are attached to criticism. Studies from teachers have shown that a 3:1 or 4:1 praise-to-criticism ratio is good.[4]

How and When Will I Deliver This Feedback?

As mentioned, a key issue in virtual feedback is the lack of synchronicity. You have to work harder to give feedback quickly in a virtual setting.

How

The *how* of delivery is critical for making sure your recipient hears your feedback well. If you want to deliver clear feedback, notes are critical. In this new world, it makes a lot of sense to write down your feedback immediately. There are two reasons for this:

1) Obviously, you need to remember exactly what you wanted to say. Laying out your comments, with examples, will help you make sure you don't forget any salient points. There's nothing worse than vague criticism or praise. How are they supposed to know what to do next time?

2) Notes also give you a chance to review. You can check your language in your notes before the meeting. Are there hot-button words? In retrospect, do the complaints and/or praise seem reasonable?

I like to keep the notes going at all times so that when appraisal moments arise, I have specific examples and a pattern of behavior noted.

To be clear, I am not speaking against the idea that you should give feedback immediately, but what is *immediately*? You must be able to frame issues by taking a bit of time to make sure you are saying what you need to say in the most useful way possible and also to make sure your own emotions aren't coloring the situation too much.

Research shows that many managers don't correctly assess the feedback they give, thinking they've been very clear, when in fact, the recipient hasn't absorbed the information in the desired way. This failure to communicate might come down to the *illusion of transparency*, which describes the idea that people are so focused on themselves, their own feelings and emotions, that they overestimate how much other people are receiving the information they are putting forth.[5] Basically, we humans assume people can read our minds. A helpful way to avoid this way of thinking is just to remind yourself of this bias! From another study, managers who acknowledge and understand that the evaluations they give to employees are not perceived in the same way by the employees deliver more accurate feedback, diminishing the gap between the two perceptions of the evaluation.[6]

On a practical level, it's often better to use videoconferencing (versus phone or email) for serious feedback, so that you can use your physical self—in particular your smile and voice—to soften and modulate the criticism as needed. How you say things is just as important as what you say.

Another study looked at two groups: the first where participants received negative feedback but accompanied by positive emotional signals, defined as nodding or smiling, and the second where participants received positive feedback but given with negative emotional signals, frowns, and narrowed eyes. Recipients whose positive feedback was accompanied by the negative emotional signals reported feeling worse about their performance than participants who received negative feedback accompanied by smiles or nods.[7]

For a different approach, a phone call may seem less "serious" if you call employees out of the blue and thus may minimize the threat response. So, depending on how threatened this person may feel about the conversation, you can dial up or down the formality of the medium.

To close any formal feedback session, ask employees to paraphrase what they heard. Multiple studies show that employees often hear much more positive feedback than managers think they delivered. On a practical note, with bad connections and distractions afforded by not being in the same room, you can't literally be sure they heard what you wanted to say. By asking them to paraphrase and return the feedback, you can narrow the gap between both of your perceptions about how they are performing. Paraphrasing also cements the ideas for them.

Asking them to paraphrase also gives you a great opportunity to understand their nonverbal messages related to the feedback. Where do they dwell or spend time when stating the citation, and what do they gloss over? Allowing them to speak not only allows them an opportunity to have a voice in the discussion but also allows you to better understand how they felt about the criticism. This approach can either help you deliver more effective feedback later or understand how to treat them in the coming days. If they are feeling extra angry or saddened by the feedback, you can give them space to deal with that on their own time, or find an opportunity to focus on alternate strengths.

Employees who are stressed about their "failures" often have a hard time finding ways to improve. You want to put them in a place where they are mentally ready to get better. Using their nonverbal cues to guide their behavior is a critical step in this process.

You can also follow up via email with any parts that you don't mind writing down. Written feedback tends to be taken much more seriously, so it's important to use the follow-up email with discretion. But there are times when you may want to underline the points you made or key areas of improvement that you want them to reference.

This approach aligns with knowledge distribution in a remote workforce; it's important to document things that need to be referred to repeatedly. If there is—and I hope there is!—a playbook for the task you are critiquing, adding these criticisms in the form of things to note or remember in the playbook is another helpful way to document the opportunities for doing a great job.

When

The short answer to *when* you will give feedback should always be "quite soon." Preferably in private and not in a tense situation, unless necessary.

The long answer has many more nuances. Particularly, you'll want to weigh the desire for immediacy against the tension of a situation.

Determining the time is a little easier when the feedback is positive. Let's say a colleague does a team presentation over Zoom, and they smash it. Here are three options for providing feedback:

- You can quickly Slack them to tell them what went well.

- You can make mention of it the next time you're in a one-on-one discussion with them.

- You can write a longer email with very clear examples of what they did super well. Bonus points for cc'ing your boss.

Each of these has benefits and circumstances where it's appropriate. You could also do all three when someone doesn't do quite as well at their presentation, but would you want to?

When you must give negative feedback, you must prepare yourself mentally. As we discussed in Chapter 1, "Improving Your Own Empathy," your state of mind is critical to being able to deliver information empathetically to your team. When people hear feedback, they often assign more weight to it than the person saying it does. As I covered in the earlier chapter, you can only behave at your best empathetically when your own energy and mental state are covered. So make sure your attitude is as even-keeled as you can manage. Have a snack, drink some water, and take a few minutes to relax.

For timing and communications tool considerations (such as phone versus videoconference), it's good to think of this feedback as a two-axes situation: immediacy versus intimacy. In the idyllic office world of yore, you could give immediate, face-to-face feedback. Because that approach is off the table now, if the feedback is immediate and minor, a less stressful approach is to have it be less intimate, such as a quick Slack just after receiving an email with a point you want to correct. If the feedback is larger and requires waiting, it's better to lean on a more intimate tool for conveying it, such as a video or phone call.

In situations where you have serious or complex feedback to deliver, you may want to disregard what I said earlier about prefacing your communication by asking if you can give them some feedback. As I said, the problem with this approach is that it's a rhetorical question; you don't want an answer, so asking it can be a little condescending. But if you think they'll need a minute to prepare for very serious feedback, then it can be a good introduction. This way, you give them time to prepare, and you create a neutral zone to frame your comments as feedback, not criticism. This approach also creates *cognitive scaffolding*, which makes it easier for them to hear the feedback. They are expecting it and understand how feedback works from all their past experiences, so they can put the feedback into their collection of previous experiences and protect their sense of self as needed.

This approach can also make some people feel outmaneuvered and then defensive. This doesn't mean you should avoid using this opener; it's a very popular piece of giving feedback for a reason. But it's important to think about how this opener might affect the listener.

How do you give someone a virtual, office-appropriate hug after a crappy presentation? Do they want help doing better next time, or do they know what went wrong and not need you to rub salt in the wound? In a remote work situation, they can, of course, hide their emotions much better. And if they have another meeting afterward, they can turn off the video and stew. And if they don't, they can go for a run or find a punching bag to blow off steam.

This is the time for humor if you know the person well—a GIF or joke or emoji to let them know you're thinking about them. You want to be open to discussing and moaning about the situation. But they don't have to join in if they don't want to.

In an office, the physically nearest friend could have been the one to do this, but in a remote meeting, there might be more people who this person could easily confide in. Remember, while it *can* be you providing the shoulder to proverbially cry on, it doesn't *have* to be you. You don't want to shove your concern down their Slack.

Praise or Positive Feedback

Positive feedback is the greatest tool in any human being's toolbox of empathy, digital or not. Everyone *loves* to hear nice things about themselves. Praise creates a feeling of kinship. It makes the recipient like the giver more, and it helps people better understand their strengths and try to cultivate them.

Whenever you have an opportunity to praise someone authentically, you should jump on it. There is so much that can be said about praising people, and most of it has been said more eloquently than I ever could. I wholeheartedly recommend Dale Carnegie's *How to Win Friends and Influence People.* The book is obvious, outdated, cheesy, and folksy, and it barely fits with many of our current cultural norms. And yet, it is still brilliant almost a century later. He explains how to be charming in a very effective and concrete manner.

To be concrete and concise, praise is useful for four reasons:

- It makes people like you.
- It makes recipients happier.
- It makes them better at their jobs.
- Giving praise makes you happier too.

Let's explore how these benefits work for you.

It Makes People Like You

Praise also reflects well on you, thanks to an effect called *spontaneous trait transference*, which is the idea that if you communicate a specific trait about someone, it becomes associated with you. These associations last over time and can be both positive and negative. So giving someone positive feedback, both to them and about them to others, reflects well on you. You want and need your team to at least respect you, if not downright like you a lot, to inspire cohesive strategy. If you are brilliant, then you can get by on respect alone. But let's assume you're a step or two below genius. It really, really helps to be liked by your team.

It Makes Them Happier

Research tells us positive communication correlates with much higher worker engagement. Focusing on employee strengths increases engagement at work far more than focusing on weaknesses. Receiving recognition is also strongly correlated with engagement, as well as retention.[8]

Neuroscience has even shown that people process verbal praise similarly to receiving a financial reward.[9] What could be better?

To take advantage of the benefits of praise, you need to keep it ongoing. In addition to giving off-the-cuff praise, schedule time, at least once a year, to really think about what people on your team are good at in a broader and more consistent sense. I recommend putting this both in writing and a phone or video call. Hammer it home.

In Glassdoor's Employee Appreciation Survey, 53 percent of people said "they would stay longer at their company if they felt *more* appreciation from their boss"—even though 68 percent said "their boss already shows them enough appreciation."[10] The lesson? More is better.

Another well-known business tenet—that praise should be public—takes on another facet in the WFH world as well. Shining a positive spotlight on your team makes them feel appreciated, but this is harder to achieve in the digital world. How many company or departmentwide Slacks just get ignored in the deluge? Consequently, you need to be very concentrated and thoughtful when you give out this praise, so that it's not just noise. You want your bragging to be succinct, to the point, and tied back to the business's success as much as possible. And you don't want your praise to be demanding of people who don't want the spotlight. It's one thing to note someone's success briefly in a meeting or firmwide email; it's another to drag them onstage and make them give a speech about what has happened.

Another surefire way to inspire people with positive praise is to email someone higher up a compliment about an employee and bcc or forward it to them. Everyone wants to know their superiors are talking nicely behind their back.

It can be hard to know what remote colleagues are doing, so finding ways to make praise public and persistent is great not only for those being praised but also for those who are motivated by being the next to win the accolade. Making praise visible is also a great idea—giving people a visual example of what success looks like, such as golden headphones or specific "gold star" Zoom backgrounds that team members can "win." This type of visibility is tied to the transparency and documentation necessary in a remote or hybrid office. Praise needs to be shared and available in the same ways that culture or playbooks are. Not necessarily using the same mediums, but an effort should be made to make sure these instances of positive feedback are public. What works for one team may not work for another. Each culture will have different ways of giving acceptable public praise, so tapping into what has worked in the past and then giving it a fun, technology-advanced spin will allow you to capture the spirit of intimacy with the communications at hand. Surely, technology will evolve to meet these needs of teams as remote work becomes more entrenched, so it's good to keep abreast of what options your commonly used tools have to issue public praise or awards.

It Makes Them Better at Their Jobs

Praise is also really useful feedback, because it lets people know what to lean into. If you are good at something, you are likely to want to do more of it and receive even more praise. A virtuous circle!

The best praise is specific and clear. People don't always know what they are good at or how it appears to those around them. Being very specific in your praise is useful for giving people a clear understanding of their strengths. It's also useful for calibration, to help them understand that you see them as better than other examples you've seen in the past. Such praise might involve notes on the best-delivered parts of a presentation, where their emphasis and delivery really hit home with the listeners. Or it might be looking over work output and conveying how clearly they achieved the required task with regards to a business goal, such as a sales report that makes it really clear where each team has room to grow for a specific type of sale. It's great if this praise also captures their growth in this area, since it's nice to know your efforts to improve are noticed.

Praise is even more important for star performers. Great performers are the most likely to take feedback and use it to get better. A Japanese study showed that receiving praise after a simple finger-tapping exercise led to greater skill gains than not receiving compliments; the praise actually made the participants better.[11] When you think about working from home, with less opportunity for bonding, praise is something that managers can give out that really can make a difference in someone's day.

Giving Praise Makes You Happier Too

Happiness researcher Shawn Achor has found that sending praise to people actually makes us happier and increases our social network. Giving others positive feedback improves your outlook on life.[12] And your ability and willingness to provide feedback is what defines you as a manager. If your role is to get the best out of your team, making sure they know what they are doing well and what they could be doing better will drive your success. Mapping this skill to a remote workplace takes additional thought, but feedback is an area where almost everyone can continuously improve.

Your feedback is one type of knowledge that you must disseminate. In the next chapter, we talk about the other types of knowledge that need to be disseminated in an office.

CHAPTER 6

DISTRIBUTING KNOWLEDGE ASYNCHRONOUSLY

DISTRIBUTING KNOWLEDGE IS A big part of corporate life—the communicating of information from person to person and group to group across the organization. When we move to an all-virtual or hybrid workforce, we lose a lot of the richness of communication, as well as many of our opportunities to communicate in real time. These are the nuances that allow humans to experience, interpret, understand, and act on pieces of information beyond words. While communication is different in a virtual or hybrid setting, it's still possible to retain and even expand on this richness—with the right adaptations. Transforming our communication styles for a hybrid workplace provides a critical benefit to the evolution of work.

Good communication in any setting gets the right information to the right people at the right time—and at the right level of complexity. In other words, you are distributing knowledge to others. Having a distributed workforce puts more onus on creating communication tools that allow for rich, asynchronous, complex communication of ideas and actions. And it's a key opportunity to upgrade your team's abilities, as 75 percent of organizations surveyed in Deloitte's 2020 Human Capital survey say, "creating and preserving knowledge across evolving workforces is important or very important for their success over the next 12–18 months."[1]

For example, distributed workers require more transparent communication to keep work output flowing when real-time communication is impossible. You can't always communicate in real time, so all of your comms must be held to a higher standard.

How do you begin implementing the changes necessary for effective communication in a virtual setting? This is a conversation ideally between management and IT/information systems, but even if you can't effect change at the organizational level, there are always opportunities to better use the tools you have.

In this chapter, we focus on the necessary facts, actions, and strategies of your asynchronous communications—as opposed to the more deeply interpersonal, which we covered in relation to listening in Chapter 1, "Improving Your Own Empathy," and from a different angle in Chapter 5, "Giving Feedback Online."

Let's start with an example of when I didn't manage these communications so well. Early in my career, I needed to implement a global sales training and learning program. This project involved deciding what information the sales team needed to know, designing a curriculum that allowed them to learn that knowledge, and developing a testing system to make sure everyone's knowledge was at the right level. While sales, sales operations, product, and marketing leadership were broadly on board with this effort, the implementation was largely left in my hands.

In this global organization, I had a better relationship with some sales leaders than others, often based on time at the company or geographic proximity. Different sales teams also had different levels of product knowledge, commensurate with the demands of their markets. And, of course, everyone has different ways they like to learn information. I could probably write another book on what I would have done differently in this example, but here, I focus on the three biggest issues and how solving them is important for virtual teams.

I wasn't transparent enough with leadership at the outset. I needed them to both direct the vision and check my work, and without the buy-in of directing the vision, they were less likely to want to check my work. If they had checked my test before I sent it out, we could have saved ourselves a lot of regional heartaches. Since we were all in different offices and time zones, we couldn't get in a quick huddle anytime someone brought up a valuable question. But the one-to-one emails I received with valuable feedback were directed at me, or worse behind my back, not allowing for the ideas to be widely shared or improved upon. I should have provided in-depth documentation, ideally via different channels, to allow them to absorb the information both on their timeline and in a way that felt most comfortable to them, whether that was meetings, video recordings, or written documents. And then, they should have directed the feedback to open channels, to create a space where the project could improve communally.

I also didn't give the sales teams enough time to get used to this idea. Again, we were not in the same room ever, so it was hard to get a post-meeting read on how well they digested the information the first time it was presented to them. The idea of being quizzed on work struck some as condescending. Dripping this message out slowly, while getting feedback, would have made this pill easier to swallow and also given it the credence that would make them *want* to pass.

Lastly, and probably most importantly, because I wasn't sitting face to face with the people this project would impact, most notably the salesforce, I thought of them like chess pieces. I didn't behave empathetically, thinking how my communications would land on their plates, either in meetings or in emails. I was very top level—telling them what was coming but not providing much context. I had failed to put myself in their shoes and consider how these changes would impact them. It was naive of me not to consider how this change would be perceived by those around me. I needed to help them realize that what I was doing was not only good for the business but also good for them. I needed them to know that I had their best interests at heart and wanted to put them all in a position to succeed.

I assumed they would know I was always thinking like this, but that's foolish. You can never assume other people can read your mind, especially when they haven't participated in the same strategy sessions you have or had access to all of the reasons why a change must occur.

I also assumed that the sales organization would be comfortable with some level of uncertainty. I had a top-level plan for how the learning program would work, so I was confident it would work out; but I hadn't really thought through some key day-to-day aspects. This practical implementation is particularly key in virtual instances.

It wasn't possible to get inside the team's heads and *know* how they would react to this information, but I could have asked myself a few questions, anticipating their responses:

- Will this be a lot more work?

- Will it be thankless work?

- Am I taking them away from something they really enjoy?

- Does this put them in a position to be seen by management and to shine, or are they being relegated to what could be perceived as the "back burner"?

- Since it affected a sales org, the number-one question always is, How does this affect their commissions?

Chess people are all well and good in theory, but that's all they are: a theory. Real businesses have real employees, and you can't just expect them to change their skills, relationships, or desires overnight.

Why Do We Need Knowledge Transfer?

The example I shared is probably not a surprise to anyone reading this book. But how do you practically implement solutions so that your organization is always maintaining and sharing information effectively? It's critical for running a business, as research shows Fortune 500 companies lose at least $31.5 billion a year by failing to share knowledge.[2] Researchers in the field of knowledge transfer look at institutional and organizational memory:

- The knowledge of what employees have done in the past, as it relates to the institution (or parts of the institution such as teams and divisions)

- The site-specific information; for example a team in the US might approach a problem one way given what's happened before, but a team in Tokyo would have no experience of how the NYC team did it.

Situational memory was and is a big driver of knowledge, but its limitations were blown wide open in the pandemic. And now, in a hybrid workforce, you are likely to have further location asymmetry, with some people in the office and some not.

To share your ideas in a team environment, you must consider how to optimize for asynchronous communication, especially in global teams. How do you begin?

At the outset, for example, you will want to set cadences for communications when working together, such as a weekly report everyone contributes to, so that at some points in time, you are all on the same page. When people are working in such a decentralized fashion, having these fixed points of information can anchor everyone and provide external deadlines as motivation.

But cadence isn't the only thing that matters; consider the culture you are creating in your new hybrid world. The gold standard should be to create a culture of idea and information sharing: to make all the information people need available, both at a glance and more in depth. One study showed that salespeople who were encouraged to seek advice from a randomly chosen partner during structured meetings had average sales gains exceeding 15 percent. There's concrete value in distributing knowledge across a firm.[3]

In addition to concrete value, what do you get from a culture of idea sharing? The benefits include the following:

- Helping employees solve problems more quickly

- Getting new employees up to speed faster

- Facilitating the creation of new knowledge

- Fueling innovation

- Deepening client and customer relationships

Multiple scientific studies back up these benefits, such as one from an auto repair firm that tested providing checklists to mechanics. Revenue was 20 percent higher while using the checklists! The authors noted that the "checklists appear to boost productivity by serving both as a memory aid and a monitoring technology."[4]

What Constitutes Knowledge That Needs to Be Shared?

When we think about asynchronous knowledge transfer in a company, it can take many forms:

- Updates about a project shared in a meeting and then transcribed into notes and shared more widely

- A playbook on how brand guidelines are adhered to

- A recorded Excel training class given by the learning and development team

- And everything in between.

To best optimize for a hybrid workforce, you need to figure out what knowledge needs to be institutionalized first and then how to keep it up to date. While there's an ideal world—where everything is kept up to date—realistically, involving too much process will slow your team and result in limited marginal returns. Given the benefits (such as those listed) from implementing a better institutional knowledge policy, you can prioritize those that are most important to your org. Then, within those benefits, you can determine which documents, playbooks, and so on, would be the most helpful.

What Good Knowledge Distribution Gets Us in Terms of Empathy

In general, knowledge transfer helps create transparency, which contributes to psychological safety and a feeling of certainty. In the brain, uncertainty is perceived as a gap or an error, something to be corrected. Until this error is corrected, you can't feel comfortable. That's why people crave certainty; not knowing what will happen next requires you to focus on this error and look for solutions to create certainty, thus wasting brain energy. The opposite situation, where you are a master of different tasks like listening to music while jogging, allows you to use energy more efficiently. But the moment something unknown enters the picture, like a pedestrian stumbling into your way, this gap or error needs correcting. You're no longer listening to the music; your threat response is triggered, and all your energy is focused on correcting. In short, you don't want people constantly diverting their energy to creating certainty at work because it takes away from other things they could be doing.

Giving your team the opportunity to learn from you through knowledge transfer is a part of management. As a manager, you are expected to have more experience and knowledge, to have more opportunities to make changes that benefit the business. Another benefit of sharing your thinking behind decisions made is giving your team insight into your inner workings and an understanding of how you process ideas. Giving your team the opportunity to learn from you is a part of management. In addition, you're giving them the opportunity to better understand who you are as a person. In your mind, how do you get from point A to point B? Allow them to harness empathy too! If your team is effectively noting how your mind works and learning how and why you make decisions, they can work better with you and potentially apply what they've learned to their own careers or leadership path. This goal of transparency could almost be seen as *reverse empathy*, putting the team in *your* shoes.

You may have noticed I said you should make sure your team members "feel" they know what you are thinking. No one can ever truly know what anyone is thinking, and it's naive to think as a manager you're going to share every thought. It would be irresponsible and unprofessional to share some information, such as another teammate's poor performance and subsequent bonus. Thus, the goal is not 100 percent transparency, but 95 percent transparency. Focus on giving the information necessary for the team to feel connected to the business's wider goals and key strategy. This way, the team has a feeling of purpose, a reason to come in and do the job they are doing. Without this feeling of transparency and shared strategic thinking, they are just cogs in the wheel. They are also less likely to share ideas that could prove pertinent or even revolutionary, but for the purposes of this book, I am focusing more on the *feelings* of transparency than the concrete benefits. These ephemeral benefits are critical in maintaining the motivation of your team.

How to Think About Asynchronous Knowledge Transfer

Asynchronous knowledge transfer, as I mentioned before, means you need to hold all of your office communications to a higher standard, because some portion of any in-person communication, the nonverbal cues, will not be there to provide additional data points for the recipients. Being thoughtful about the different levers you can pull for all of the knowledge you are disseminating will give you a framework for building a culture for asynchronous communication.

Considering What You Are Communicating

Considering what you are communicating is the first framework for thinking about important pieces of information you need to make public, whether they are about your company's culture or a new merger. This framework defines how you think about the communication knowledge distribution levers discussed later. All of these must be rooted in empathy, if they are to be used correctly. The point is not whether the information is important to you; it's about whether the information is important to your team. That also affects how you think about who needs to know the information and what it means for their time horizons. Consider the following questions:

- How important is the message?

- Who does it affect?

- What is the time horizon (none, immediate, long-term)?

Let's look at my example from the beginning of the chapter. It affected a lot of people, had both a short- and long-term time horizon, and was of medium importance. If I had thought about those three factors in advance, I could have better revealed my plan to my collaborators and the sales team.

HOW IMPORTANT IS THE MESSAGE? Unsurprisingly, *importance* is the most crucial of these factors when you are transferring information in the office. How great an impact will this piece of information have on people?

This measurement can be considered for ideas both big and small. For example, if the parking lot will be closed for a week, that's probably not as big an issue for the whole organization as 10-percent layoffs, but both are extremely important to convey to the people who need to know. You have to think about ideas that cross your "desk" and need to be filtered out. How thoroughly should you think this through? How much time do you want to dedicate? The answers will have a big effect on formality, richness, and repetition, which we cover later under the axes of communications.

WHO DOES IT AFFECT? The question of who needs to know has many facets. First and foremost, it's a question of transparency. You want and need to keep the right people in the loop on any decision process, and if they can't overhear you speaking casually about projects and ideas, you need to be more formal about communicating what you, your team, or your org is working on.

- Consider first the practical level: who needs to be in the know because they are responsible for actions?

- Then consider who needs to know because the actions will have a knock-on effect on these people. Upper management is an example.

- Finally, consider people who may not need to know but may *want* to know—out of curiosity or a desire to grow their own roles.

Gossip is also a key factor when considering who knows something and asynchronous communication. People in an office talk; this is inevitable. You, I am sure, already know to assume that nothing can stay a secret. Take this consideration into account when disseminating information. Particularly in a virtual work environment, conversations are either totally private, such as over the phone, where no one else can hear; or they can be essentially totally public because emails can be forwarded, many meetings are recorded, and so on.

These issues bring up a unique dichotomy of a hybrid or remote workforce. On the one hand, transparency is key to being able to work well in a distributed team. On the other hand, as everyone knows, too many cooks in the kitchen are never good for a project. We talk about this issue more when we think about *richness* as an axis, because layers of information allow you to keep everyone informed without letting too many opinions derail the nuances of a project.

On a practical level, technology is rapidly developing to help teams decide who has access to what information, when, and to what degree. Note taking and project trackers, whether on Excel or an Asana or Jira board, are ever more critical in capturing the relevant background information, discussion topics, and action items so that people not in the room, virtual or physical, during a discussion can be kept up to date. Nothing takes the place of synchronous communications like meetings; they are clearly one of the best ways to generate ideas and actions within a group. But if having everyone in the same time zone or space isn't realistic (and it rarely is, anymore), our processes must be designed to keep the information flowing.

WHAT'S THE TIME HORIZON (NONE, IMMEDIATE, LONG-TERM)? The time frame before the action must occur and how long the impact will be felt afterward also affect who you tell, when you can tell them, and the transparency involved. In my earlier comparison between the parking lot being closed versus 10-percent workforce layoffs, the necessary time horizons both for communicating the change and how long the change will be felt are quite different. Assuming there's other reasonable parking, people may need only a few days to understand this concept and make sure that everyone who needs to know where to park knows. If you're talking about something as serious as people losing their jobs, the time horizon for impact might be much longer, but you probably won't tell many people until right before the layoffs.

Time horizon planning also allows you to give people the opportunity to think through problems with you, not only because they might have very valuable suggestions to offer, but also, once again, to make them feel as if they're a part of the process. People are more committed to processes and changes that they feel invested in. This process-oriented approach is critical in building upon that feeling of transparency.

When you share upcoming process changes with employees, there is not only shared ownership but also shared workflow. You want your team's ideas and help in thinking through problems to get the best diversity of thought and drive the best results. But the process of shared thinking is also about building the team's confidence and skills.

A lot of institutional knowledge has a longer-term horizon. It may be a year before you need to review the budget again holistically, and thus, a playbook for budget reviews won't be touched again for another ten months.

When to Pull Which Knowledge Distribution Levers

If you know who needs to know, how important knowing it is, and the time horizon for knowing it, you can use the following levers to get your information to your team in the most expedient fashion:

- Platform
- Durability
- Guest/Access List
- Cadence
- Richness
- Formality

PLATFORM Where you host the information is critical. Given the many technology companies trying to solve this problem, I won't go into my personal experiences and risk dating this section practically immediately. Suffice to say, when considering the five other levers, they should give you a guide as to what platform, with its inherent benefits and drawbacks, would be best for hosting and sharing which types of knowledge. We also discussed platforms such as Slack, email, and document commenting in Chapter 3, "'Speaking' So Others Will Understand," which also gives a helpful perspective on platforms and mediums for message delivery.

DURABILITY How long does the information need to be accessible? The accessibility will vary on a spectrum:

- From very fleeting content like a random Slack message that will effectively disappear from the stream except if searched for
- To a pinned Slack
- To a printed handbook you put on everyone's desk

You want to make sure that you don't overuse the most durable communications for messages that don't need to sit around in print form. You equally want to ensure that information needing to be referenced repeatedly receives the appropriately long-lasting home.

GUEST/ACCESS LIST When someone can't see what's going on, they might assume they're being left out—that other people are making all the interesting, strategic decisions without them. And work from home takes this to another level. It's all too easy to forget to invite people to meetings or copy them on emails when you rarely, if ever, see their faces.

The onus is on everyone in an organization to combat that kind of behavior and create a culture of inclusive information by being very thoughtful and even a little overly organized about sharing information.

An easy way to solve this issue on projects is keeping a RACI chart, listing who's Responsible, Accountable, Consulted, or Informed for each item. If you're using software to track projects or OKRs (objectives and key results, a style of goal setting made known by Google) to track goals, this RACI information should be baked into the process. This way, everyone knows who needs to be included and, before scheduling a meeting or sending an email, can refer back to this information to double-check their list of recipients and make sure the right people are included.

This question of who needs to know what when can lead to some issues with what information to include in one-to-one or side meetings, in my opinion. You should make sure that going over the projects at hand doesn't contribute to asynchronous information sharing. If you find yourself giving one person an update sooner than peers or stakeholders, it's important to note that exchange and quickly follow up with the others via email or phone to keep everyone on the same page. An example would be if you're waiting for funding go-ahead from the board, you get favorable but unconfirmed information from an unrelated meeting, and then happen to go directly into a one-on-one with a relevant direct report and share this "gossip." If you don't share that information somewhat formally, say via Slack to the relevant group, you risk playing favorites simply because of communication styles and cadences.

As it pertains to access, there's a trend now toward transparency that every company will have to weigh. Do you want to make salary information available to all? Some companies have. Sharing this information can be great for trust. It's also important to consider your own approach to transparency—including whether it needs modification. Some organizations could benefit from transparency, depending on the type of workforce, their demands for transparency, and local regulations. Others might find that too much transparency foments discord and doesn't allow management to take the top-level strategic decisions they are paid for without having to sell them across the entire organization, thus wasting time educating people beyond their need to know.

CADENCE How often will you repeat the information being shared? Actions such as having everyone reread and then re-sign antibribery terms or the employee handbook every year are knowledge events you know you will repeat. Maybe in every team meeting, you will also want to look at progress toward goals. Or you'll announce the budget; although it's written down in a durable manner, you may formally announce it only once to the wider team. But hopefully, you won't have to announce layoffs every year, so that issue wouldn't have the same cadence.

Cadence also affects the platform and guest list. Different required cadences can be baked into projects, with some people getting more frequent updates and others less frequent ones.

Another concept to be transparent about is letting people know the cadence in advance so that they don't have to worry about getting updated or left out.

RICHNESS How much effort will you put into the medium of the message? Anyone who has seen the ninety-seven-slide culture manifesto from HubSpot or the annual culture book from Zappos can tell you that some documents are better for having more effort put into them. These very impressive pieces of knowledge tell a story to employees and outsiders about how much the company values what they are conveying. But that doesn't mean there aren't instances when a simple two-line email isn't perfect. There are several ways to cut the spectrum of richness, and for many projects, there might be more than one right answer. A team working directly on a project launch would want access to a detailed project plan, whereas management would need top-level insight only on a monthly basis, with the possibility of looking at the project plan if they are so inclined. Again, how important the message is—along with the audience—is critical in deciding the richness of any communication.

Video is richer than text. I expect to see more recorded videos used in internal communications as we progress further into work from home because videos are both intimate and easy to distribute asynchronously. In 2020, US adults spent 103 minutes per day watching digital video on devices,[5] so while this is not the most common way to convey messages asynchronously, as I write this book, I think it will become more and more commonplace as people's media habits permeate the workplace.

One element of richness that can often be forgotten in a virtual or distributed workforce is *affiliative social engagement*. This term describes the moments when people, in person, see others moving to the rhythm of the music, when everyone applauds together, or when a crowd laughs at a funny joke. Studies have shown that while this moment in time increases people's feelings of engagement with those around them, it doesn't have to be in person to work. Virtual noises from others, either in real time or prerecorded, can produce the same convivial effects.[6]

Richness is also impacted by the meta information stored with any knowledge; for example, who was last to update and what changes did they make? For some types of documentation, this information is critical and should be a factor in deciding what platform to use.

Richness also comes into play in celebrations. While I was at the *Financial Times*, we reached a significant subscription milestone, and someone filled the lobby with helium balloons signifying the number of subscriptions. That's a different type of richness, the wow factor, which is great for conveying excitement without having to type a lot of words. The Google home page, with icons designed to celebrate different calendar moments and milestones, could also serve as inspiration for a virtual way to achieve the same wow effect, like having IT remotely change everyone's desktop background temporarily to celebrate big news.

FORMALITY Because almost everything needs to be scheduled in a remote work environment, sharing knowledge casually is harder now. The medium, your word choice, even your apparel if you choose to do a video message—all convey a level of formality. Different office cultures approach formality differently, and generally, the corporate world is becoming less formal, but considering this issue is still useful if you're giving an important message the respect it demands. Messaging tools, such as Slack, are generally a little more informal and useful when the tone you are trying to convey is more of a water-cooler moment. A letter that appears at everyone's home is the opposite—very formal and usually reserved for statements from your retirement account. But that doesn't discount the idea that one time, you may just want to send beautiful letters to everyone on the team to commend them for a job well done.

Knowledge Distribution During Onboarding

Onboarding puts all other knowledge sharing to the test. It's a crucial time to set the stage for the employees, your team, and the company. Ask yourself: "What do new employees encounter when they begin with your team?" This is both a practical question—where do the new starters find the institutional knowledge, contacts, and information necessary to do their job?—and a cultural question—what kind of environment are they (virtually) joining? What will they need to know to do their jobs effectively and feel they are a valued part of an important team? While not all of this information sharing is asynchronous, it often is predominantly so, at least from the perspective of the manager and the new hire. So we consider it from this angle to make sure we cover the most critical or difficult implementations.

How Do You Onboard Effectively in a Virtual Office Setting? The Practical Side

First, you will need to give answers and offer solutions after asking: "What do you physically need to do your job?" Obviously, anyone working in this setup will need functioning tech, a laptop, email, and so on. After that, I think the real key to success is a workplace that is well documented—where everyone can see the goals, the teams, and the processes, simply and intuitively.

Of course, the more rigorous your structure is around documentation and training, the easier it is for everyone to do their jobs well. But this effort to be transparent and well documented can help with onboarding. Take companywide transparent OKRs (Objectives and Key Results) or KPIs (key performance indicators); they make it very clear for a new starter where the organization is heading and who's in charge of what.

The basics for onboarding involve having all the documents new hires need for their job ready to go, including an organizational headcount chart and a plan for how they'll spend their days. Following are some best practices involved in onboarding someone in a virtual setting.

ONBOARDING PRACTICE 1: FIND AND SHARE YOUR APPLICABLE DOCUMENTS Run through the processes and operations this person will encounter, and try to collate all the necessary documentation as well as possible, if you don't already have this information in order. Who has access to the important documents and why? When were these documents last updated meaningfully? Which ones are important? There's a lot of digital clutter in all of our folders, and every new starter (assuming they aren't coming at you too fast!) offers an opportunity to see which documents really serve your needs. In an ideal world, your documentation culture would be such that a new hire wouldn't cause much of a blip. But even in the best of circumstances, a new hire is an opportunity to stress-test your documentation and knowledge distribution system.

ONBOARDING PRACTICE 2: CLEAN UP YOUR CALENDAR, ESPECIALLY AS IT PERTAINS TO YOUR TEAM You want the new hire to go through each meeting they have with an understanding of the purpose of every meeting and those attending in their first month on the job. It's a good time for you, as the hiring manager for this role, to look through your schedule and figure out which meetings of your own are relevant and which might benefit from a refresh, and then ensure they each have useful agendas/Slack channels/ working documents.

ONBOARDING PRACTICE 3: UPDATE YOUR ORG CHART An up-to-date org chart is a good start, but does it show who's working on what? I'd love to see a world with interactive org charts leading to a kind of internal Myspace-esque page (am I showing my age there?) for each employee, with a little about each person. Most critical from a business standpoint would be a clear explanation of what each person is working on; who they work with; and any public KPIs, dashboards, or goals. For the purposes of networking and team cohesion, I'd also like to see a clear photo, some fun facts or personal photos, and the like, to create a 360-degree view of who they are. This more robust org chart helps new starters remember who's who, figure out who to go to for questions, and better understand how things get done.

ONBOARDING PRACTICE 4: GIVE THE NEW STARTER A GUIDE What are they going to do on their first day? Their first month? Sitting all day in a Zoom call is tough. Why dump more meetings than necessary on your new starter?

Training should include a mix of group meetings, formal learning, one-on-one meetings, and self-directed learning. I like to think of these training options as a series of to-do lists, linked to each of the first four weeks on the job. You should give new employees as much clarity as possible, while allowing for flexibility—such as a list of people to meet the first week, then the second week—allowing them to schedule these meetings themselves. And this guide also allows for agency over their days, so if they have a necessary two-hour video call, they don't have to follow that up by watching two hours of training tutorials.

One idea I've heard—which, for some roles, I thought sounded useful— was assigning the new hire a "fake project" to give them something to start working on immediately. Possibly a project that's been done before—to give a concrete structure to their work, allow them to ask the real questions, and discover who to ask for what in a less stressful but more structured way.

Of course, let them know that the project is not "real" but is for the sake of learning and prompting important questions.

ONBOARDING PRACTICE 5: HAVE THEM TAKE NOTES There are two ways to think about taking notes. First, as a new hire goes through documentation, you should ask them to flag anything that is unclear, is laid out in the wrong order, or could have been done better—anything that would make the process easier or more clear. This information would ideally benefit subsequent new hires.

The second goal is to use their fresh pair of eyes to benefit the whole team. Having them take notes will give you their perspective on your operations in general. They should be looking critically for general opportunities for improvement—ideas that could be simplified or are outdated compared to other places they've worked. It's great to get someone with limited knowledge to look over your work and highlight issues and ideas you aren't seeing. It's good to get their reflections immediately but also again a few months later, because with time, they might better understand why a choice was made in one way or another. Secondarily, this exercise also allows them to provide value early on and reveals what kind of feedback they like to give—a key insight into their workplace behavior and attitude.

How Do You Onboard Effectively in a Virtual Office Setting? The Culture Side

Besides the practical items, the second type of knowledge you transmit to a new hire is culture. Unsurprisingly, sharing this information comes with a different set of challenges compared to traditional business information. In addition, a virtual workplace makes culture communications more complex.

So why is it hard to explain culture in a remote environment? As work culture evolves, particularly post-pandemic and other elements of social upheaval, new hires are going to expect a more open and welcoming workplace, and onboarding is a good place to start. We can design onboarding that strengthens teams, enhances positive behaviors, and makes newcomers comfortable and productive. However, there are challenges, particularly remotely, that need to be overcome:

- Most people find it hard to define "culture."

- Most companies, while they may have explicit values, haven't thought about how these trickle down to culture.

- In a remote environment, the trickling down of information can either get lost or take on outsize importance depending on the situation.

- Culture has all too often been used as an exclusionary social tool to make people of different backgrounds/beliefs feel out of sync with their peers, and this, rightly, makes people fearful about being too prescriptive with culture.

Despite its roadblocks, culture plays a critical role in employee engagement and retention.[7] It can help unify a team and share the story of who you are as an organization.

Your goal is to make new hires feel as though they can fit in and become a part of the team. You could also say this is just good manners, welcoming people by giving them transparency about the cultural codes they can expect.

It's worth asking relative newcomers as well as "old hands" what they think the cultural outliers are, the actions and habits they see in common office behavior that don't jibe with the stated culture, to understand where you might need to be explicit about what people can expect in their new work life. Like so many things in a virtual office, culture needs to be more explicit. *So write out a manifesto or a playbook for it; spell it out, to make it easier on people.* This manifesto should convey what the organization's strengths and focuses are in a way that makes it clear what behaviors could contribute to those strengths and focuses.

How to Onboard: Making New Hires Feel Valuable, Involved, and Included

How do you get someone embedded in the human side of being on your team, the "social fun" of work, so that they are engaged in the culture? There are four stages of bringing someone into your team: supplying home office swag before starting, introducing people, conducting a welcome "party," and continuing to socialize.

PHASE 0: HOME OFFICE SWAG Without a physical office, we've lost the cognitive scaffolding that makes up work. That is to say, a lot of the clues that tell your brain, "I'm at my employer space now. This is who they are and what they stand for, and this is the acceptable behavior within these confines." All this has departed with COVID-19. How do you rebuild this?

Swag! You want employees to be positively reminded of their workspace, with a way to make it personal and comfortable, as well as on-brand. So beyond the perks of good office tools, great branded items that serve as visual reminders can also provide that office context. But this is not an invitation to get junk printed with your corporate logo. If an item won't provide value and isn't something you'd be proud to have on your desk, *don't do it!*

Some ideas:

- Branded versions of any of the new WFH necessities, like laptop stands, keyboards, mousepads, the basics of a home office
- A laptop case
- A coffee mug or water bottle
- A desk calendar (We all know it's hard to pay attention to time when the days seem to blur!)
- Great pens or pencils (maybe with a choice, because we all have preferences between rollerball, color, and so on)
- Sticky notes (Possibly it's just me still using these to keep track of my ideas!)

PHASE 1: AIDED INTRODUCTIONS Now it's time to introduce your new hire with as much context and structure as possible. Your first step as the manager is to make the big announcement of who they are and what they'll be working on, whether your introduction is emailed, Slacked, or whatever is customary to the rest of the organization. An introduction can feel awkward for new hires, so the kindest way to approach it is for you to draft a version given the format your company usually uses—such as with a photo, with or without too much personal info—and then let them edit. If appropriate, you should extend this intro to social media as well.

To introduce them to their colleagues one on one, start compiling a list of who they need to know well before they start, ideally put together by the person departing the role. Put these introductions in order of priority, with some background so the new hire goes in prepared to take in the information they need relevant to the relationship.

I've previously suggested the idea of everyone on the team creating a slide about themselves or a fun collage about their outside-of-work self. But I know this approach can make people uncomfortable because it feels too revealing, so you should suggest it only if your team is ready for it. If it feels appropriate, it can be a great memory tool, assigning a more robust background to people you meet and making it easier to connect with them, both on the first meeting and in later interactions.

It's good to have a set agenda for these meetings, maybe even with an icebreaker to help share personal information that feels okay for work. Two truths and a lie, what you wanted to be when you grew up, ideal vacation— all of these are great opening questions that allow people to share without stepping over their intimacy boundaries.

PHASE 2: WELCOME PARTY Having someone new starting at the company is a great opportunity for some forced fun! It's a great way to cement ongoing team relationships, give the newbie an insight into the bonds between different employees, and break up the normal cadence of work. We cover virtual team building further in Chapter 4, "Driving Real Connection with Your Team."

PHASE 3: CONTINUED SOCIALIZING Now is the time for *continuous, asynchronous, forced fun*. Sounds academic, right? Ha! A great example of this is Donut, the Slack bot that matches you up for coffee chats with random colleagues. In general, people should be free to make their own relationships, but they will still benefit from a guide to randomly sort their options. And for low-intimacy relationships, having some framework to break the ice and make the act of digital relationship building feel less forced. Other examples of continuous, asynchronous, forced fun include video conference bingo, screenshotting funny things you unintentionally are shown in a videoconference (e.g., the same outfit two days in the row or a Christmas tree still up in late January), other competitions like finding the best meme of the week, or a meeting-free book/TV series club where you all watch/read at the same time but don't have to discuss together all at once. Refer back to Chapter 4 for more details.

Creating opportunities for bonds to form between employees without management pressure is critical for well-being but also for skills transfer. One Harvard Business School study of a mobile phone factory showed workers often shared their "tips and tricks" for assembling phones more effectively than the official methods. But these experts were noticeably more likely to give these informal lessons when they weren't concerned with too much management scrutiny.[8]

THE (IDEAL) END RESULT: NATURAL FUN Hopefully, all these efforts in onboarding lead to natural fun, pleasant relationships among colleagues—and a new employee who feels embedded in the social aspects of their team.

How to Embed Knowledge Distribution in Your Culture

All of the ideas in this chapter on knowledge distribution are intuitive to anyone who's accustomed to office culture. If they thought about them, they would know intuitively these are the right ideas. It's the implementation of them in a hybrid or virtual setting that matters. How do you make a great knowledge distribution culture an innate part of your team and not an impossible ideal? Here are four important points in summary of this topic, which will get you well on your way to instilling knowledge distribution as a part of life for your team:

- *Make it important.* Management has to agree that clear process documentation and knowledge distribution are imperative. As hybrid work comes for many corporate roles, it's a perfect time to effect these changes and put structure in place to ensure they remain in place. But everyone has to believe in these changes. Gaining support is hard if management doesn't believe in remote work, but if they do, it should be an easy sell. What works for remote work is also, largely, what works for hybrid work, at least in terms of knowledge distribution. Earlier, I gave an example of the study of the auto repair firm in which the use of checklists increased revenue by 20 percent. Despite the revenue boost and the commensurate commission boost from their usage, the mechanics did not use checklists of their own accord, only with the firm directly monitoring their use.[9]

- *Make it a habit.* Until they become part of your team's routine, checking on knowledge distribution, calling people out for falling short, and rewarding those who are committed to keeping processes and documentation up to date are tasks a manager needs to attend to frequently, as much as weekly or biweekly. This focus will also allow you to cut the efforts that are more hassle than they're worth, which surely some knowledge management does end up being.

- *Make stress testing a habit as well.* New hires or people cross-trained in different roles can reveal documentation holes. Surprise questions about the state of a project from upper management might also have this effect!

- *Prioritize the right technology.* All the Asana boards (digital project management tools) in the world can't keep everyone up to date all the time. Particularly after reading and digesting the frameworks for thinking about knowledge in this chapter, it's a good time to evaluate which technology pieces are working for you and which are not. The outcome of effective knowledge distribution is more important than the technology, but it's still important to get the best tool for the job, if possible.

Knowledge distribution is your greatest opportunity in a virtual office. Transparency and clarity lead to better processes and better outcomes, and being forced to tackle these priorities in regards to institutional knowledge will separate great virtual companies from the rest. It's not the average manager's job to make sure that the company institutes all the necessary technology and processes to drive this success, but everyone can make it a priority within their team.

CHAPTER 7

DISTRIBUTING KNOWLEDGE SYNCHRONOUSLY: WHAT DO GOOD MEETINGS LOOK LIKE?

IN A REMOTE WORKFORCE, for many people, meetings *are* work now. They *are* the office. One of the primary channels by which to synchronously transfer information or knowledge with a remote team is through meetings. They are the scaffolding of corporate life. They are the most common mode of synchronous communication in a modern office and have proliferated in many distributed teams.

After the start of the pandemic, the average worker was spending up to 25 percent more time in videoconferencing meetings than before.[1] Thus, we must approach them seriously, as energy drivers, time drivers, and culture drivers.

The reasons for this explosion of meetings are practical. Without the chance to run into people and solve issues quickly, meetings are necessary to get people's attention and find solutions promptly. They are also critical for transparency, because any attempt at grabbing someone quickly often results in information asymmetry. This method might have been okay in the office when everyone had equal opportunity and access to the person sharing the information, but now with hybrid teams, this approach leads to bottlenecks and lack of trust. There might also be a bias toward appearing busy. When your manager can't see that you're working, a busy calendar gives the appearance of hard work.

In general, these meetings aren't always run well. One report suggests that 78 percent of workers say their meeting schedule is always or sometimes out of control.[2] Besides the schedule, many other aspects of meetings can go awry.

Following is a framework for thinking about all the facets of meetings, including the type of meeting, goal, cadence, agenda, roles, physical format, attendees, and actions for after the meeting. With this framework, you can set up your team for success, using meetings wisely and effectively to get the most out of everyone's time.

Why Do We Have Meetings?

As I said before, meetings *are* the office for a remote team, and they are necessary for successful teamwork. But that doesn't mean you want to spend all day in them.

The point of a meeting is to congregate the necessary parties to share information in real time and allow for back-and-forth. Meetings also allow real-time debate, which can cause ideas to flourish. One study found that pharmaceutical development teams were better able to learn from another team's experience when they invited members of another team, those holding on to the institutional knowledge and experience, to actively participate in their meeting. Actively contributing to problem solving—as opposed to just sharing information in a static, asynchronous fashion—created better outcomes.[3] Meetings are also theater, a stage to allow people to show off work they've been doing or their standing in an organization. Creating an effective meeting culture should result in happier employees and higher productivity.

In the 1970s, *Harvard Business Review* published a classic treatise called "How to Run a Meeting," and a lot of it still holds true. My favorite line is, "In the simplest and most basic way, a meeting defines the team, the group, or the unit. Those present belong to it; those absent do not. Everyone is able to look around and perceive the whole group and sense the collective identity of which he or she forms a part." It's this idea that creates the definition of meetings as remote work; it's the purest moment of collaborative work.

When we think about meetings as a type of knowledge transfer, some of that knowledge is concrete work stuff, but a lot of it is social. Again, from HBR's "How to Run a Meeting": "Since a meeting is so often the only time when members get the chance to find out their relative standing, the 'arena' function is inevitable. When a group is new, has a new leader, or is composed of people like department heads who are in competition for promotion and who do not work in a single team outside the meeting, 'arena behavior' is likely to figure more largely, even to the point of dominating the proceedings."[4] This theater of meetings is one of the reasons that, despite all the best advice in the world for how to effectively plan and run meetings, they can still run amok. We need to acknowledge this human need for attention and interaction and build our meeting plans around it. In a remote office, where the chances to peacock your skills are less frequent or communal than they were in an open-plan office, meetings will naturally serve this function. Making sure there's an outlet for this behavior can often help to create order in a team's meetings.

What else do we need to consider when switching to remote meetings? Of course, you don't have to travel for them, and you don't have to wear trousers. Most importantly for the business of getting work done: in Zoom meetings, you can't interrupt as easily, and there tends to be better adherence to agendas.

How to Have Better Meetings

Given the importance of meetings in the modern workforce, you need to have a framework for thinking about their purpose and formats, to ensure you're using your and your colleagues' time wisely. The following are some concrete best practices.

Define Your Meeting's Goal

The first question you must answer about meetings on your calendar that are taking up your precious time is, why you are having them? What is the goal of these meetings? Spell out this information for the team. It's ideal if the goal is tangible and tied to the business goals and revenue, but that's not always the point of collaborative work. It's okay to have goals that are not results-oriented in the typical project or revenue sense, but if you can't link your meetings back to goals or revenue at all, then you should probably ask why you are hosting them. Great reasons for team meetings include getting everyone to share what they are working on to

- effect collaboration
- reduce repetition
- and inspire creative thinking.

But this works only as long as everyone walks into the meetings knowing that. The goal for your meetings should be in the calendar, along with the agenda, so everyone knows what they are getting into.

Categorize Your Meetings

Meeting goals fall into four categories. By understanding the goal and category of your meeting, you can make better decisions about the agenda, attendee list, format, and so on. The four types of meetings are tied into their purposes:

- *Inform.* The purpose of these meetings is to provide updates to the team—information that people need to know. General team meetings and all-hands meetings fall into this category. When you are setting the agenda, informing colleagues should be your north star. These types of meetings can be recorded and watched at a later date, although attendance is beneficial for camaraderie (as are the inevitable side conversations—more on that later).

- *Recap.* These check-ins are not so dissimilar to informative meetings, but they are for a specific project or idea, usually making sure everyone is on the same page. This type of meeting particularly applies to people who have been less involved in the specifics or day-to-day aspects.

- *Create.* These meetings have a very clear process and action item: to come up with new ideas. The format, technology, and physical location need to be set up with this goal of creation in mind, to create the output—whether that's a project management plan, an entirely new product idea, or a set of OKRs.

- *Decide.* These meetings have one purpose, and that's to help you walk away more clear about the outcome of a decision than when you walked in. For that reason, they almost always require significant prep work so that people can have all the information at their fingertips. Roles are also hugely important because someone needs to keep their eyes on the ball and ensure the team is working toward a decision. If a decision can't be made in the meeting, the team can assign necessary action items and define the timeline to decide at a later date.

Decide Whom to Invite

Seeing meetings as an arena or a performance puts that interpersonal dynamic into the right context. The knowledge being distributed might be as much about the players as the words they are saying.

Deciding which team members to invite was also covered under "Guest/Access List" in Chapter 6, "Distributing Knowledge Asynchronously." But being more selective in a business that needs to cut down on meetings is generally a good idea. Being selective is easier if you are clear on the category and goal of the meeting and can then decide who would most benefit from being in the room. And if asynchronous tools for knowledge distribution are functioning effectively, that puts your organization in a great position to share updates without taking up precious meeting time for everyone who might want to be informed.

There is a flip side to this, as referenced earlier when describing meetings as an arena. People often want to be invited for status or interpersonal reasons that aren't best for the business. This is not necessarily a bad thing; we can't take innate human desires out of our efforts entirely. Trying to decide whose perspective will matter the most, whom you can easily appease, and who you don't want to piss off—these are all challenges for an empathetically minded leader to take on. Your goal is to manage the business aspect ("Let's achieve our meeting's goals.") while also managing the human aspect ("How can I best work with the involved parties?"), both in this meeting and in the long term. Clear agendas help with this task, in that they can also mention who's invited and why: "Meeting to discuss learning and development budget for 2023, with a goal of top-level allocation . . . Attendees: functional department heads to decide allocation, senior management for visibility, and HR business partner to offer guidance." With a clear idea of each person's contribution, you can more easily convey why you don't need more attendees from HR unless there's a specific reason why additional guidance would help to allocate the learning budget.

Cadence! Decide How Often and How Long to Meet

One study says a full third of meetings are unnecessary.[5] It's a huge waste of time to sit in a useless meeting. Not to mention, workers who feel they spend too much time in meetings report decreased well-being, increased fatigue, and increased subjective workload.[6] Therefore, your goal should be to make meetings shorter and less frequent; you want to cover what you need to and no more.

Cadence is also about energy, how often specific meetings repeat, and how often people have to repeat the same information to different parties. You don't want multiple meetings with similar goals happening repeatedly. When in doubt, use a larger meeting and have people join in and drop off. If you're being very clear about the agenda, you can get more of people's time and attention. However, doing so can be complicated if you don't set up a culture of actually leaving when your time is up. It is even worse if you show up at a meeting unannounced and make comments when you're not supposed to be there. There are technological solutions to this issue now, and surely there will be more, but how you handle these details comes down to culture. In all cases, you must be firm about a culture that respects people's time. Other ideas include the following:

- Set the default on your calendar to be shorter meetings. Can you get the information across in twenty minutes? Aim for the shortest time possible.

- At the end of each meeting, confirm when you need to meet again, if you do at all.

- Use a timer. Timing your meetings can be a delicate balance because unstructured conversation with your colleagues is sometimes a nice part of work. And sometimes, it's an unnecessary irritation. Timing works better for larger meetings, where it's more understood that you are trying to move quickly through the relevant topics. And be sure to have a solution for topics that require further discussion, whether it's a specific addition to the agenda or a mechanism to extend the time equitably.

Determine the Physical Format

The physical format is unique, depending on your circumstances. With hybrid teams, the options for physical formats increase exponentially and should be thought out. Previously, having everyone sit around a conference table was the gold standard for meetings, but this is obviously no longer the case. Do you want creativity sparked by physical movement, like a walking meeting; or brainstorming, where you stand up and place sticky notes on boards around the room? Do you want the formality of a classroom-style setup? Do you want to make it easy to see everyone's face and hear their opinions?

All of these options are possible, both remotely and in person, but require a thoughtful approach to the limitations of the technology and the guest list. You can still have standing meetings remotely. And you can have walking meetings both remotely and in person. Obviously, these approaches work better for more intimate meetings where not a lot of information has to be written down, but the upside is that they are more energetic and can get people out of a thinking rut.

When talking about information transparency, a good idea for team/org meetings is to establish a very clear repetition of sharing—forcing different people or functions to present something, however briefly, every time, to keep all the ships at sea aware of what they are working on. In my team, we always did one-minute updates at our biweekly all-marketing meetings (with, I might add, a timer).

If some portion of the team is in the office and some are at home, use the best layout for equity. Balancing the desire for those in the office to have that camaraderie without leaving out in the proverbial cold those who are dialing in is a complicated effort. At a bare minimum, the audio should be set up so that everyone has equal access to the conversation. That means if the conference room isn't wired with good speakerphones, people should take the call separately until that problem can be fixed.

Create an Agenda

What's the format of a good meeting? One that follows the agenda! Routines can cause people to glaze over, so it's not a question of laboriously sticking to the details, but finding the right way to cover the items on the agenda. In fact, research has shown that having or not having an agenda has no impact on the perceived value of a meeting.[7] It's not enough to have the agenda; the purpose is to create a goal for the meeting and then be transparent about what you'll need to discuss to achieve that goal.

The agenda should cover not only what you'll be speaking about but also, if you can, the order of and approximate time allocated to those discussions. The agenda keeps things moving at a nice pace and also gives people a feeling of control and agency. In the same way that physical spaces carry implicit meanings, a schedule provides scaffolding for people to understand what's coming when. But be aware: the order of the agenda is a form of bias—we overweight the first topics discussed[8]—so keep that in mind when designing the agenda. As mentioned earlier, you should also note who is attending and why. Letting people know explicitly why they are needed for a meeting is not only good for culling the guest list but also is a kindness. Often, senior leaders are invited to many meetings, just for visibility. If you make it clear when attendees are needed to give guidance, make arguments, or arbitrate, they can more easily prioritize their schedules.

Short meetings are possible only if everyone comes prepared. Having short meetings is great in a hybrid workforce, where we should all have more time for focused, solo work and where we can prepare for our meetings in advance. Agendas need to be clear and thorough, assign ownership, and provide links to supporting documents.

Agendas should also be as clear and rich as possible within the constraints of time. If you're vague and write "training budget," you are not very clear about what's going to happen in the meeting or why people need to attend. If you write, "To discuss the proposal for an increase in next year's training budget, who should own it, and where it should be allocated. The goal of the meeting is to have rough allocation determined with a concrete allocation and ownership due next week," then everyone can come ready with their arguments and views.

The ideal for many meetings is an agenda with supporting documents. You don't want any part to be just like last week. Otherwise, you are wasting time. By including documents or reports that anyone can check in advance, and the responsible parties can highlight the important parts, you can keep the discussion flowing more effectively. Even better, put the salient facts in the agenda as well, then open up the meeting for discussion or move on quickly.

AGENDA FORMAT An engaging digital work environment is built on the right energy and cadence of the day. Spicing up your format can make your meetings more interesting. I would add a caveat and say that adding layers just for the sake of making it interesting often does not make the meeting interesting. Only when these options contribute to the overall goal of the meeting do they actually create a beneficial contribution to people's energy levels. The agenda is another opportunity to consider the meeting from everyone else's perspective. What are they walking into? Clarity is a kindness if you are asking someone to give up time that they might prefer to use for something else.

In my team meetings, I like to have each attendee give one-minute updates. We go around the room and let everyone briefly share, without interruption, what they are working on. Their update has to be one minute! This way, people can see what others are working on, follow up later with things to contribute, find intersections and opportunities for collaboration, and just feel heard. The key is that the update is brief, equal, and one-way. If you start interrupting, the meeting quickly becomes a free-for-all. This updating technique is also equitable, in that everyone must speak and no one can hog.

Technology in this space is always evolving, but in general, digital tools to break up the meeting, allow for brainstorming or intimacy, or allow for more inclusivity (such as polls, breakout rooms, or quizzes) change up the format of meetings and keep attendees on their toes.

For smaller meetings, where you have the opportunity to humanize your colleagues, you ought to leave time for chitchat at the beginning, particularly in interviews, but really in all calls—something to remind us we are all human. Maybe one person can share a certain type of anecdote, like the best thing they ate last weekend or the most bingeable show they are watching right now. Regarding energy and respecting people's time, however, if you don't want to waste time on things like this, it's an important balance of what is quick and what feels right for your team. We should also remember that this kind of chitchat was normal originally, but WFH has pushed us toward more efficiency, and some of that behavior has dropped off.

Assign Roles

- Chairperson
- Note taker
- Shut-it-down person
- The good manager (that's you!)
- The crowd (that's everyone!)

Meetings need roles—if nothing else, at least a chairperson and a note taker. It's important that the role of chairperson is not always an actual leader, but an opportunity for leadership for anyone in the team. This role can rotate by meeting or by quarter, but for large meetings, it's critical that someone is in charge of the agenda and timing adherence.

The note taker is an underestimated role. As all historians know, what actually happened and what someone wrote happened are not necessarily the same thing. The job can seem thankless, but in a distributed team, it's important to capture the salient points of a meeting so those who couldn't attend are able to understand what happened. To avoid the historian's bias, rotate this role and, if possible, have as neutral a party as possible take on the task.

Another key role is the "shut-it-down person," who's ready to end the meeting when the goals have been achieved. In some organizations, shutting down meetings might be unnecessary or rude, but in many, meetings run longer than they need to. While the chair should be in charge of sticking to the agenda, having another person—perhaps more removed from the purpose of the meeting yet confident enough to jump in—is useful in giving everyone time back. Meeting lateness, the idea that the meeting runs over and into time reserved for other activities, has been shown to be "negatively related to both meeting satisfaction and effectiveness," so taking steps to combat this time bleed is critical.[9]

Lastly, your role as a manager is to model the behavior you want to see. Videoconferences, like any meetings, are opportunities for people to model the behavior of others. If most people in their little Zoom boxes appear to be attentively listening, you probably will be too. If, on the other hand, most attendees have turned off their video or simply joined without video, you are less likely to reveal yourself as well. While I'm not committed to every meeting being a videoconference, if it *is* a videoconference, not turning on your video prevents rapport building, decreases the cohesiveness of the call, and essentially looks rude.

What do you do about side conversations among the crowd? It is totally normal in larger meetings for there to be side comments and commentary, some professional and some not. Imagine hearing a presentation on a new product feature and quietly turning to your sales partner and mentioning a client. This product could be a really great fit given what they told you in your last meeting. This is a great aside and a part of working in an office. Or imagine some sniggering when someone makes an extraordinary Freudian slip during their quarterly update. That's just human nature.

How do you build these side conversations into a videoconference? This is a really tough question, and the answer is still up for debate. Of course, many people take their eyes off the video screen often, but that's not something generally to be encouraged. They are then missing information, and if they leave and go into Slack to see the funny aside you've sent, they're unlikely to ignore other messages and return right back to the call. You can try taking your inbox offline and composing emails quickly, making sure to give the correct context because, of course, they'll be receiving the message later and may not remember the context. And this doesn't really deal with the example of an LOL at the Freudian slip. This camaraderie and casual information sharing may just be lost for now, but hopefully, these exchanges can come from other sources. And hey, at least the person who made the slip isn't getting laughed at anymore!

Circulate Meeting Recaps and Notes

The point of taking notes is to store them as part of the organization's institutional knowledge. There are four concrete objectives for meeting notes:

- Update people who weren't able to attend.

- Record meetings so that you can reference responsibilities, achievements, and comments.

- Store the action items.

- Take a "roll call." If you have an issue with people missing meetings, particularly those who require decisions, you can add this information to the notes. Its ostensible and perfectly proper purpose is to call the latecomer's attention to the fact that they weren't there for a particular decision or discussion. The sneaky effect, however, is to have a public record of those who missed this moment, to either change their behavior or to have a record if you need to make the point at a later date.

Continuously Optimize Your Meeting Culture

One key foundation for a great meeting culture is making sure you're soliciting feedback and being transparent about your aims. This is a key part of a hybrid company's culture, so you must make it clear: What is your team stance on video calls—is it video on by default or sound off? What's the purpose of using video over just phone?

Soliciting repeated feedback, say quarterly or biannually, for what could be better in meetings allows team members to be more inspired and effective. You then can optimize the necessary schedule for the team. For every metric or lever in this chapter, you should be transparent with your team about why you think this is the right cadence for a meeting or how you thought about it. Back to using empathy to define your leadership, you want to give the team a feeling of ownership over a process that will really impact them. Being glad you have a "shut-it-down" person is easier when they cut you off after you've voted on the idea and agree with its value.

Meeting technology will continue to evolve as we move further into a remote working world. But the tenets that make meetings useful don't change. We need meetings because we need to see and hear our colleagues thinking and arguing in real time. This is one of the primary avenues of community decision-making in a business. When we move this effort to virtual formats, we may have to be more systematic in our processes, but the output should be the same. Putting frameworks around opportunities for group synchronous communication can help us all disseminate information and make decisions faster, more equitably, and ideally with better results, no matter our location.

CHAPTER 8

GETTING SOMEONE TO QUIT

How to Get Someone to Quit

Poor performers exist; this admission won't come as a shock to anyone reading this book. And when a poor performer must be moved off a team, suffering occurs on both sides—often with a protracted, HR-driven departure process.

But there is a better way. Using empathy—seeing the situation from the poor performer's perspective—allows you to help them leave of their own volition. Warning: this technique requires a lot of effort and compassion, but ultimately, for everyone involved, it's the best way to remove poor performers from your team.

You want a poor performer to want to leave on their own terms—and not because you made them feel too miserable to stay. You want to respectfully show them why moving on would be better for them, as well as the team.

Jack Welch put it best in his book *Winning*, sharing how the best way to help poor performers move on is with a "no-surprise, minimal humiliation approach."[1] Walking out on one's own two feet, as quickly as possible and with as little drama as possible, is one major silver lining of remote work—in that it is easier to slip out quietly and intentionally when working outside of the physical office.

Not everyone will take your olive branch to depart without drama. But more often than not, the olive branch is never offered—at least not clearly or with enough intention. Instead, I've seen poor performers subjected to more than one formal performance review. Usually, having multiple reviews is a sure sign that this person is in a bad place in their role. If they continue as if nothing is up—increasing their level of performance to the bare minimum not to get fired, but not actually improving to an acceptable level—this is where I think managers can do better. I want to lay out a system for how to do so.

The hardest part of my role as a manager is dealing with poor performers. Back to Kim Scott's book and the idea of *ruinous empathy*—being too kind to people, too careful of their feelings—it can be really hard to separate not wanting to hurt someone's feelings in the short term from the long-term cruelty of letting them flounder.[2] So when I feel someone doesn't have the capabilities needed for the job, I want to walk through these questions as I consider my next steps:

- Is it just me?
- Is this person wrong for the role, this team, or the company?
- Does this person know they are underperforming, or could I be better with my feedback?
- Are they happy failing?
- How do I fix it?

Is It Just Me?

Asking "Is it just me?" is a key moment for empathetic perspective taking. It is impossible to be unbiased in our opinion of someone. Numerous perception biases cloud our thinking, despite how aware and conscientious we try to be. So, the first thing to ask yourself to determine if this is an issue that extends beyond you is, "Are they actually not good for our team or organization, or do I just not like working with them?"

How do you figure out if it's *just you*? Usually, if someone is awful to work with, the whole team thinks so. And likely, others aren't shy about making that opinion clear—subtly and not so subtly.

Sometimes, though, people are on the fence, and you don't want to create a culture of soliciting negative feedback about people's peers. That creates a *Lord of the Flies/Survivor* mentality where people are encouraged to tattle, which is hardly anyone's idea of a psychologically safe place to work. This feedback about peers should fit into your general formats and platforms for soliciting feedback, to ensure that it's a normal pattern of behavior that sometimes surfaces negative, along with positive or neutral, information. Some organizations have success with 360-degree reviews, though making them positive and effective while not too onerous for the participants requires a lot of dedication and effort.

As you determine how the rest of the team feels about working with this person, you can observe interactions. Team meetings and outings can be great occasions to subtly understand connections and camaraderie among individuals—essentially, *who likes who*. In the "olden days" in a physical office, recognizing this dynamic was easier. Just seeing where people sat and how they arranged themselves when unstructured could give a lot of clues.

It's still possible to pick up on these connections and emotions in a remote team. I think the best digital clues are evidence of unnecessary collaboration. Here are some observations you may make:

- Are team members working together on projects that might be a little outside the scope of their day-to-day work, and are they keeping each other abreast of activities outside of their required check-ins? These are signs of people who want to connect with each other and get great things done.

- Conversely, do they need to be reminded to connect on projects that another person needs to know about? That's usually a sign that someone isn't gelling. Do you notice a trend in who people are avoiding?

- Does this person seem to get left off communications or invitations?

- When you solicit positive feedback—say for quarterly "shoutouts"— does this person's name come up often and from a varied cohort of people? Or do they get skipped over, time and time again, by everyone on the team?

Using your digital empathy skills to try to understand how other people react to this person can be a clue that perhaps you aren't alone in seeing their underperformance.

Another option is soliciting feedback from the team in a nonpunitive way. This communication could occur either in 360-degree evaluations or in post-project feedbacks, where everyone either highlights top performers or gives everyone a score for their efforts and additions to the project. When you can't see people working together, these tools give you insight without calling out one person to provide additional feedback about someone—which could feel like an "I gotcha" game. These tools can also help you learn the dynamics of how projects get done and who is responsible for what output. As we move toward increasing transparency and accountability in a hybrid or remote-first workforce, this understanding of how productivity occurs—and between which team members—becomes even more important in designing high-functioning teams.

Is This Person Wrong for the Role, This Team, or the Company?

If you've ascertained the problem is not just you, next you must ask: "What are the circumstances here that aren't working?"

When you're not physically working with someone, it can be hard to tell what the issues are. Sometimes, someone is smart and great to work with, but they aren't working on the right projects or tasks. And sometimes, they just don't fit at a company and are struggling to get things done for cultural reasons.

When you have determined that you are not the reason for the problem, what are the possible options?

1. They can be coached, and they will improve.

2. They can be coached, but they won't improve.

3. There's no point in coaching, since they are such a mismatch.

4. There is something going on in their personal life that is causing an unexpected blip in their performance.

It's your duty to test out opportunities for improvement, letting them know exactly what success would look like. It's also your duty to understand whether something happening in their personal life is driving this problem. If this is just a blip, it's better to retain someone during a lull in their effectiveness than risk wasting time hiring someone else, only to find they are actually worse.

Perhaps this team member hasn't learned how to do their job properly, which means they may need additional training. It's also possible they are unmotivated or just aren't a good skills fit. Establishing their strengths and weaknesses will make it easier to gently guide them toward a role that works better for their skills—even if it's outside the team or organization.

Is it the team? Perhaps the person whose performance is suffering has the same abilities as someone else on the team who comes with other advantages. Perhaps the other person performs slightly better or is more experienced. If the struggling person has a good rapport and reputation within the company and you have someone who can take over their role, is there anywhere else in the company they could go where they might shine?

If they culturally don't fit, that can be the hardest to deal with. Culture is the hardest to hire for and the hardest to fire for. How easy this situation is to deal with depends on the person's level of self-awareness. Do they sense that they don't fit? If so, and if they show empathy toward themselves and the team, then it's likely just a matter of time before they will want to move on. If they don't perceive this mismatch, finding a way to let them know is incredibly delicate.

Does This Person Know They Are Underperforming, or Could I Be Better with My Feedback?

First, if someone on the team doesn't know they're underperforming, it's probably your fault. It's on the manager to express dissatisfaction when necessary, so that people can right the ship and perform at the top of their game. But let's assume in this example that you have done everything right and this person *should* know they are underperforming, but they don't seem to.

In short, you must *improve your feedback*. As Mark Twain (supposedly) said, "If the first thing you do each morning is to eat a live frog, you can go through the day with the satisfaction of knowing that that is probably the worst thing that is going to happen to you all day long."

Regardless of who made this statement, for me, feedback is an "eat your frog" job. That is to say, it's mentally draining and needs to be cleared from your to-do list as a priority. I try to think of it like this: *it's psychologically taxing for me to tell someone what they are doing wrong, but it's the kindest thing I can do.* What communication techniques would be helpful to this person? You can test out a few specific ways to improve your feedback and coach an underperformer.

BE CLEAR As you give feedback, make it very clear how they could improve. Share specific examples they can see, focused on behaviorally specific descriptions of what you want done differently. That could include taking notes of specific word choices that convey a bad attitude, screenshots of work that is not focused enough, and so on, but examples that prove the point simply. There's a fine line between proving your point and beating a dead horse. You don't want to present a laundry list, which can make them feel attacked. A singular example isn't great either because it can leave room for excuses ("Oh, it was just that one time.") and may not put the person in the mind frame of needing to fix it. Using three examples is probably about right.

PAINT A PICTURE OF SUCCESS A lot of people prefer metaphors to understand concepts that are unclear to them. They want to have a full view of what success would look like. The more 360 you can make your picture, the easier it may be to understand. For example, find a way to show how the output, the time it takes to do it, the initiative, and the stakeholder relationships all play a role in what success in this job looks like. They may not be seeing their coworkers' success and realizing how far behind they are falling if they aren't tracking their own output versus that of others. Especially in a remote workforce, this visibility must be intentionally created.

As an example, say you have an employee named Joe who needs to present a plan to the budget committee to test out a new piece of software. You might want to say, "Joe, here's what a really good job would look like, and one that I think will convince the budget committee to okay the plan. First, a well-researched proposition, with both qualitative and quantitative research backing up your proposition. Talk to at least ten people, both inside the company, customers of your support, and at the supplier, to paint a really clear picture of the benefits. Then add your comprehensive financial model that spells out numerically why we should do this. Lastly, make a killer presentation, no longer than twenty minutes or twenty slides, both visually appealing and compelling. I can help you find resources and practice so that the presentation is really good. That's what it would take to really do well on this project."

COMPARE THEM TO OTHERS Comparing employees can be risky, but for some, competition is an amazing motivator. Studies show that rivalry in the office, as extrapolated from NBA teams, drives more success.[3] Competition increases physiological and psychological activation, which prepares body and mind for increased effort and enables higher performance.[4]

Competition can elicit two types of emotions. For some people, it promotes anxiety and fear of failure and humiliation. Yet for others, it promotes excitement. One of these, as you might imagine, is not conducive to creating an atmosphere of psychological safety.

Research shows that when people know that they are being judged against the performance of someone else, their threat response kicks in, which releases cortisol and other stress-related hormones.[5]

An example might be to say, "Joe, I know that you're making an effort to log your sales processes so we can use them for reporting, but I don't think you're at the level of effort and output I need from you. If you take a look at how Jane logs hers (with a visual example), you can see she's done X, Y, and Z, which is how I want it. Do you think you can get up to this level?"

FOCUS ON POSITIVE CONSEQUENCES While there may be a time when you need to focus on negative consequences, doing so with someone who doesn't yet know they are underperforming is the wrong approach. Embarrassing people who don't do well doesn't work. This is an opportunity to drive someone to do their best, so consider how you can excite them with the possibilities of a job done well.

For example, related to Joe's budget proposal, you might say, "Joe, this is the kind of work that will really take you to the next level, which is what I want and expect from you. If you're able to level up these types of presentations, starting with this one, I think it will be time to start developing your skills for your next promotion, starting with being selected for this leadership group for this new project (insert your own desirable yet not-financial opportunity here)."

OFFER OUTSIDE ACCOUNTABILITY Does the fear of failure need to be public, to drive employees to step into their role more effectively? If so, you can put them on the schedule to present their work to a larger group in a reasonable time frame. This outside deadline might be a good motivator. If your organization is using OKRs or other public goal setting, this is also a clear way to put someone's work in the spotlight. Make sure they have clear goals and consider printing them. Personally, I like to print my OKRs on a sheet of paper and tack them to my desk. It's easier to prioritize work when your true priorities are staring you in the face. Without an office, you may want to pin these on a group Slack or another digital pinboard for that communal visibility.

Are They Happy Failing?

People don't tend to want to be utter failures at the office, though in my experience, some don't seem to mind failing at their work tasks. I once had a person on my team who seemed utterly content with performing below the required level. They would receive negative feedback, improve their performance measurably but just not quite up to the specific level, and eventually let it slip again. As a manager, I found this behavior frustrating because I wanted to support attempts at improvement. One telling aspect I should have comprehended earlier was their attitude, a type of negative nonchalance you don't see often. It's rational to take criticism poorly—no one likes hearing their faults—but real efforts for improvement usually come with some sort of enthusiasm. Most people understand that poor performance puts their job at risk and therefore want to show their manager they understand this obligation. I should have been wary of someone who did not seem to reflect an understand the connection between performance and job security.

It later transpired this employee really didn't want this job; they had very clear aspirations to become an actor. By making them realize that they weren't in the right role, I was setting them free to pursue their dream. Remembering that *they likely want to be a success* makes getting someone out of a role they aren't performing in a much easier task emotionally. Remind yourself that in the long run, helping them move on is *truly* for the best. This is using empathy at its highest level, seeing the failure from their perspective, and believing that under other circumstances, they could do better.

Believing in their potential to be successful is a key tenet of acting empathetically. You must know in your heart that you are putting them in a position that, in the long run, will improve their life. Yet they might need a small kick in the pants to make a change and find a new role that makes them happier. (They also may not. At the end of the day, you're their manager, not their therapist or parent.)

Let's call this process *managing someone out*. It's a key trait in good leadership. It helps them, you, and the rest of the team. You cannot let poor performers fester in your team.

How Do I Fix It?

The hardest part of dealing with an underperformer is giving thoughtful, tough, critical feedback consistently and often. Step one in this process is making sure that the employee understands they are failing at their job. To find an opportunity to share this, first, assess your current scheduled feedback opportunities. If you have one-on-one meetings frequently enough, this is the time to start very clearly stating that they need to do better. You are trying to make the situation clear—for example, that there is nowhere to go in their role if their performance continues at this level.

Again, think carefully about their perspective. You are working to show them you are a manager who cares, while also making it very clear you need their performance to improve and will watch for signs of progress. They will likely be uncomfortable.

At this point, managers often get paralyzed. Managers—and really most humans—shy away from making people uncomfortable because it's easier to pretend everything is okay. In this scenario, you must lean into that discomfort you see (or anticipate) in this person and accept that it's for the best.

The hardest part of getting someone to quit of their own volition is that you are taking on a lot of the pain of this situation secretly, onto your own shoulders, for the good of this person and the good of the team. "Heavy is the head that wears the crown," as they say.

Done virtually, these calls must have you at your best, with all distractions off, on video if possible. Give these employees the dignity of addressing this situation "face to face." Despite the idea that phone calls are actually sometimes better for nonverbal cues, there is often a perception that video is a better or richer medium and confers a level of sincerity or respect.

PERFORMANCE REVIEWS AND GOALS Your performance reviews should be extremely strict, with a high bar. Set the bar where you would need it to be if you were hiring someone new. Be clear, be specific, and be prepared to be direct—and firm, if necessary. Work is something we get paid to do, and while it should be pleasant and supportive, there is no room for people who are performing lower than what the market will bear. Again, unfortunately, they need to understand they are failing, and it's your role to make that point abundantly clear. Don't be afraid to share that you are disappointed: "I am disappointed in the work you're turning in because it's not at the level I think you can deliver, and it's not at the level I need. These are some examples of what's missing. . . ." This is a very clear statement that starts from a place of how you, the manager, are receiving the information, which softens the idea of blame and makes it very clear what good or better work would look like.

To help set expectations, make sure that their important goals are incredibly clear and measurable, to keep both of you accountable. Don't make goals easy just because someone is underperforming. (Caveat: If there are personal issues, it's okay to temporarily cut someone some slack.) The bar needs to be set appropriately high so that they can demonstrate a change in behavior. Also, because you can't see how much time they are actually working, like in an office, you need some proxies for this measurement. You could make some service-level agreements (SLAs) for things like Slack response times within their core working hours to ensure that they are actually working during agreed-upon work hours, if that's part of what you're worried about. It's also pretty invasive to have a boss ask for this kind of arrangement, which can be beneficial to motivate them to improve.

MAKE SURE THEY HEAR YOU After you have provided them with feedback, do they know that they are underperforming? Do they care? Are they acting ashamed or embarrassed or checked out? Let's go back to the example of the employee who actually wanted to become an actor. Their cycle of improvement usually lasted only a month or less. That's probably enough time to tell if someone is taking the criticism on board and making efforts to change. They might need a few days to come to grips with the information and process it on their own time, but certainly not more than a week or two. And then you should see some time of enthusiastic change. Enthusiasm is different for different people; some might communicate more and let you know what they're working on. Some will just turn over better work. And some will ask if you notice an improvement. If you've set out concrete goals for improvement, it should be easy to measure progress against these goals while also gauging their sincerity about the project as measured by their own sense of enthusiasm. If they are still checked out, then you have to push further toward actually firing them, though hopefully the situation will not get that far. If they don't care about their success in the role, it's not easy to convince them to leave of their own volition. The reason is that ensuring they can find success somewhere else is part of how you would coach someone to leave (to find a better fit, and so on).

SPECIFIC, OFTEN UNCOMFORTABLE SOLUTIONS Concretely, some uncomfortable management techniques can lead people to leave a team. This happens often unintentionally, due to bad management, but these actions can also be used effectively to manage someone off the team.

As mentioned earlier, competition can be uncomfortable for people, so that's one other avenue for making someone understand their spot in the pecking order. If you tell Jim that his product presentations are less compelling than Michael's or Sue's, particularly for X or Y reason, that can paint an uncomfortable picture of how successful they are in their role, causing Jim to consider his position from that angle. Sometimes this approach works, and sometimes it doesn't, but it's worth trying.

The next step is the implementation of the dreaded micromanagement. In a more technical way of phrasing, it's time to reduce their autonomy. This approach is backed up by neuroscience, showing that reducing their autonomy should generate their threat response, as you are taking away their control or agency. Studies at the University of Boulder show that the degree of control available to an animal in a stressful situation determines whether or not the stress will negatively affect their ability to function.[6] You are harnessing this functioning of the brain and increasing their stress but also giving them the opportunity to succeed if they want to. (I should also note the opposite is true in good management: giving people autonomy reduces stress, but that's for another chapter.)

We all know what micromanagement looks like: meeting frequently to discuss how the work is going, requesting detailed status updates, checking their work, walking through ways to improve, and nitpicking over grammar and style choices. I think detailed Trello boards work really well for this; the system for laying out tasks and timelines and then seeing them move along serves as quite a stark visual message about someone's output. Sometimes, people need a proverbial *shot in the arm* to get their act together.

How they respond is key. Someone who really wants to succeed will likely be willing to put up with this nuisance to get back in the boss's good graces. Someone who is checked out will likely balk at having their work checked to this degree. Again, the best-case scenario, though unlikely, is that they do improve. Fantastic! More realistic is that they won't but that the micromanagement will grate on them.

This micromanagement creates a fair assessment of their ability and willingness to improve and is also a good way to make someone think about leaving. You are creating an environment they may not like, but this is the only way for them to succeed or realize they need to leave.

One issue with the technique of micromanaging, and the reason most people just put up with underperformers, is that it's *hard*. Micromanaging someone is a lot of work, and it doesn't feel good—for anyone. You may start slacking on scheduling the necessary meetings or going over their work with a fine-tooth comb to offer constructive but blunt feedback—all of which takes time. Again, as Mark Twain (supposedly) said, "eat your frog." In this instance, that is to say, get these tasks out of the way each day or week, early on, so they don't suck your bandwidth and motivation dry.

You should set a limit for how long you are going to micromanage, both privately and with them. You can't go on forever holding their hand. They need to get up to the appropriate level and then continue to perform without excess supervision. If they drop back down to their earlier behaviors when you remove the micromanagement, that's the same as never getting up to the appropriate behaviors. Neither leaves you with someone on your team who can get the work done and contribute effectively. Hopefully, you have time frames already set, say quarterly goals, that you can use to set a framework for improvement. That gives the underperformer enough time to make a change, but again, if you can't see a change in a few weeks, you likely are not going to see that change at all. But using your usual business timelines also creates one step before an official performance review, which usually is independently time bound; for example, "You have twelve weeks to fix these issues." This conversation should be part of goal setting and checking in with goals. "Joe, your quarterly goals have three product presentations on them. By the end of this quarter, that last presentation really needs to be at the standard we've discussed, with improvements in X and Y, for me to understand your commitment to this role. As we stand here looking forward, what do you need to make that change by the end of the quarter?" As the manager, you want to set up the employee for success, so any of these changes should be accompanied by opportunities for you to be a great manager and help them get better.

What Would Make Them Happy?

We can assume you want this person to be happy because you're a good person. Yet if having them on your team isn't contributing beneficially, you must find a new scenario for them. So away from the actual performance metrics, it's good to discuss what aspects of work they like. Help them to see that they might be more suited to other roles if, say, they love graphic design and this role is really more about email copy.

Truly consider: *what would make them happy?* You can ask which projects have been the most inspiring. Don't be afraid to be negative, too, if this person is really failing. Being too easy on them won't do them any favors. Ask which projects, in their estimation, sucked. It's helpful if projects that really annoy them are a critical function of the job, and it's not a terrible idea to drive these ideas home—how work like that is a key function of the role, so how does that make them feel? You are here to be a good manager, which in this case is getting them thinking about their next role. Keep that clarity of purpose top of mind.

Approaching your employee in this way will give you insight into their personality and wishes, in a nonthreatening way that isn't about how they are failing to perform the tasks you've laid out for them. It also subtly opens their mind up to other roles. In most places, you can't tell someone they ought to quit. But that doesn't mean you can't seed the idea of other skill sets into their brain. Usually, for legal reasons, this is a delicate path. It's really about exploring skills they enjoy, not about pushing them into different roles. But the more concrete you can be about their skills, the easier it might be for them to realize those skills aren't inherent in their current role.

I once had a marketer on my team who was, to put it bluntly, not a very good marketer. She didn't enjoy thinking about the customers, crafting messaging, setting up ad campaigns, or doing any of the other common tasks marketers take on. But she was a wizard at reading contracts that we signed with suppliers, thinking through the possible ramifications, and finding clauses that didn't fit. It was easy to see she thrived in that type of work. Over time, I made some small and some not so-small comments about this skill set and how valuable it was. I complimented her profusely on her legal-oriented efforts but also gently added that that was not the task at hand. Eventually, a few quarters of negative feedback on her actual job, combined with praise for her legal abilities, sent her to speak to our general counsel about their role and what that type of role demands. Reader, you'll be delighted and perhaps not surprised to know that she is happily now a lawyer.

This type of discussion also has the added benefit, hopefully, of softening their perspective of you. If you, as their boss, are constantly breathing down their neck about their output, you really need a humanizing opportunity for conversation. This is doubly true in a remote work scenario, where those negative interactions can be an outsized percentage of the time you spend in conversation together.

Within the confines of what's allowed both legally and at your company, this is a conversation you should have with everyone on your team. You want to know where they ideally fit—or see themselves fitting. But having this conversation just becomes more urgent with poor performers.

In the process, you don't want to put someone in a position where they feel *you said they had to quit.* That's most likely not acceptable. But you can discuss what would be next for them ideally, somewhere in the distant future. I like to talk to all my direct reports about their next job, whether it's a promotion on my team or something else they'd like to do, relatively early in our relationship. It's naive to think people will stick around forever, and if you have a great relationship, you can be honest about what feels fair for both of you. If you do this, it's a natural part of the conversation once you find someone is performing poorly.

A worthwhile approach might be to build this into a team-building session, regardless of poor performers; for example, ask, "What are everyone's best skills?" Responding to this question can turn into a roundtable of sharing positive comments about each other or a skills assessment team-learning opportunity—the type delivered by learning and development—that the team can subsequently discuss.

Why is this assessment especially valuable for underperformers? In this instance, to their ears, you may seem like more of a personal coach or therapist. Your underlying goal is, of course, to improve your team's and company's performance; but a step toward this goal is to inspire them to think of new avenues. To achieve this goal, you need to be able to really channel a high level of empathy. And sometimes this empathy can be used to help them see greener pastures elsewhere.

Once you're clear on some skills the person likes and seems to have, and that are not relevant to their current role, keep emphasizing those skills to the person when appropriate. "Don't you wish this project had more design work?" "If only you had projects that let you shine your XYZ skill . . ." and so on. Let them know you think highly of this other skill and think they would be successful if they followed it.

After you succeed in creating an environment that illuminates for this underperformer that they are in the wrong job, if they decide to leave, you should feel a sense of contentment. They have taken the first step in creating a better life for themselves, and you can look to hire someone who will be better equipped to perform on the team.

But you're not out of the woods. Usually, in this circumstance, they are likely to tell you all the things you did wrong, including why you caused them to quit with your terrible management. This is a hard moment because, in fact, you did somewhat "cause" them to quit, but you know their leaving is for the best. Do not say anything or get defensive; take it on the chin. They are leaving with their dignity; this is the ultimate goal. They may need this opportunity to tell you their story, to take back as much control as they can muster. They are looking to retain power. There is nothing for you in this situation other than to behave gracefully. Blowing off steam is helpful for people. The world is small, and you want them to leave with the most positive view of the situation possible. If that means a moment of anger, so be it. It's also better that you listen empathically, which, as we discussed, is as much about the other person *feeling* heard as anything else. This means not interjecting with your own perspective, but inserting nods and murmurs of assent so that they know you are paying attention. Statements like "I hear you" and "That's valuable feedback" let them know as well. And, of course, you want to remain calm. This situation is coming to a close, so it's time to heal the pain as best as possible and move on to better things.

Every company's and region's policies will be different, but you should keep HR abreast of these efforts at managing someone's performance and have them in the room if possible, though that is harder if the person is quitting rather than being let go because you may not know when the time will come. Even though they are leaving of their own volition and hopefully with dignity, they may also be upset, and you don't want to open yourself up to legal issues.

This is also a time to note that being overly emotional and empathetic at the same time can leave you open to manipulation. Someone else's feelings can overwhelm your own and make you forget your well-thought-out, analytical plan. Don't let other people use emotions to make you feel bad about taking the long-term position that is better for the business.

Performance management can be the hardest aspect of being a manager. Using empathy allows you to understand that letting poor performers suffer in an ill-fitting role negatively affects everyone on the team. Removing that energy from your team lifts a weight off everyone's shoulders.

SECTION 3

MANAGING CROSS-FUNCTIONALLY AND INDIRECTLY

CHAPTER 9
INTERVIEWING REMOTELY

THE GOAL OF AN interview, from the side of the employer, is to hire a good candidate who can do the job effectively and work well in the organization. There are loads of books on interviewing techniques, how to structure them, and the like. This is not that. This chapter approaches interviewing from the *interviewee's* perspective. It guides you in creating a scenario where you, the interviewer, secure the best person for the job without ever meeting them.

Like almost everything we've learned about working in a digital-first environment, there's more preparation required when you are relying on fewer visual and physical cues from human interactions. So hiring prep should be a little more involved, on both sides.

First, some introspection. Consider these questions:

- Who is the best person for the job?

- What skills are you looking for?

- How distinct are these skills? A person who understands customers, personas, and needs can probably sell in any industry with a bit of time and training. The question is, can you train them?

- What is the range of required personality traits? Are these traits you possess? What about the last person on the job?

Often, we get boxed into an idea of a role based on its previous occupants. When you feel as though you have a clear idea of what you want, you can begin looking for and interviewing applicants.

Note that this chapter is geared toward work that has an interpersonal aspect. If you are hiring for a role that is truly skills-only-based, these tools may be less effective. If you want to create an organization geared toward growth, however, you should also be hiring based on the leaders people can become, not just the work they can get done.

Here are questions to ask yourself on the hiring side, which we explore in this chapter:

- "What's the goal of the interview, and what do I need to know to assess whether this person can do the job?"
- "How can I set the stage for the interviewee to put their best foot forward?"
- "What virtual or technology format should I use?"
- "How can I avoid bias to increase diverse thinking on my team?"
- "What is my gut saying?"
- "What if they have a major technical snafu?"
- "How will I sell the role?"

What's the Goal of the Interview, and What Do I Need to Know to Assess Whether This Person Can Do the Job?

These are clearly two questions, and they don't have the same answer, so why did I lump them together? The goal of the interview should be simple: to use the next hour of your time to assess whether this person would be a good fit for and successful in the role, and then to convince them that they should want the role, all at the right price.

It's important to keep these salient thoughts in mind when prepping for an interview. Remembering these goals will drive you to uncover important details about a person. Usually, they will help you determine whether this person has done similar work before and thus would be able to handle this work, and if they possess the right type of intelligence to succeed in growing in this role.

Sometimes there are more specific goals for a role. For example, different people in a panel will ask more technical or nuanced questions that align more with their portion of the business. It's best to give the candidate a heads-up about the specific focus of particular time slots or panelists, so that they aren't thrown off guard, switching from panelist to panelist and subject to subject, without the benefit of being in the same room.

Regarding a candidate's fit, from the research I've done, most people find this the hardest component to assess in virtual interviewing. You get a much less comprehensive idea of the candidate virtually, with no clues like how they treat receptionists or what time they arrive. These indicators can be valuable. To re-create some of that human-nature component that shows up in person, it's good to leave more time than feels necessary for unstructured discussion or questions. This way, you can observe more details about how they "show up" and answer questions, interact with you, and more. A note on this: studies show that this chitchat may bias interviewers if done before the more formal part of the interview, so I suggest putting it at the end, after they've shown you they can do the job.[1]

Now for the tough part: how will you learn these things?

How Can I Set the Stage for the Interviewee to Put Their Best Foot Forward?

Studies have shown that nervous interviewees underperform and are seen to be underperforming by their interviewer.[2] This is not a reflection of actual talent, unless the job requires being interviewed in some way. You will shrink your talent pool by making people uncomfortable. Overcoming this tendency will make you a better hirer—being able to overlook some superficial aspects to find people who can actually do the work. It also will help you attract talent, creating an environment that sells the interviewee on the role.

Over videoconference or phone, you can't change your seating position to be more conversational versus adversarial, you can't gesticulate much to humanize your delivery, and you're far less able to subtly mirror their body language—a common way to create rapport. Since you've lost these and other visual and physical tools for softening your delivery, it's important to be doubly aware of how you are coming across, either on the screen or over the phone and to acknowledge that the other person has lost some of their natural charm as well.

If you are trying to harness digital empathy—which this far into this book, I hope you are—you should make it as easy as possible for someone to answer your questions or case study in the clearest way. So the first thing to do in the interview is to make the other person comfortable. Your behavior as the interviewer has a direct effect on the interviewee's feelings of ease, as shown in a study by Neil Anderson.[3] Creating that atmosphere of psychological safety, of a place that is both welcoming and demanding, is key in hiring people who will fit and succeed on your team. A 2008 study by Beth Pontari showed that anxious people perform better in interviews if they have a friend in the room.[4] While it would be pretty unorthodox to have candidates bring a friend, we can extrapolate and say that you want to be as friendly and engaging as you can to put them at ease in order to see their best, truest self.

How do you make people feel comfortable in a virtual interview? These techniques are usually used on the other side—how to make the interviewer like the interviewee—but it's a two-way street. We explore how you show up and how you want others to show up.

As in all aspects of harnessing empathy, let's assume you will arrive at the interview moment ready—with your appearance and behaviors reflecting what you want to see. When it comes to looking at and assessing body language, speech patterns, and apparel choices in others, that's a part of the interview process. These factors offer clues to how this person would be on your team, or if they even want to be on your team. Here are some points to keep in mind about what you see when you jump on Zoom.

Frankly, a little nervousness is a good thing. You want to hire someone who wants the role, who would be upset not to get it, and for most people, this tension could drive some healthy anxiety.

The same goes for appearance. Unless someone is the greatest genius of all time and nothing else matters except their intellectual fortitude, which can happen, you want to know if someone takes this interview seriously, dresses appropriately, does their hair—whatever feels right in your industry. Trying to fit in visually is a sign of conscientiousness, which is an indicator of workplace success. Let them show you they want to work in this role. But that doesn't give you free rein to focus on things that don't matter. Sometimes posture conveys confidence; sometimes it's just a quirk. How relevant is it for the job? For an outside-facing customer role, maybe it is really important.

This type of assessment is true for apparel and speech patterns as well. For an output-focused role, less so. But no matter the job, most career progressions are dependent on a person's ability to get along well with others. It's hard to be a great manager without confidence and the ability to fit in.

Your face is rather intimately displayed, often larger than life, on their screen. This advice is true for all virtual meetings, but try to have your face take up 30 to 50 percent of the screen (measured vertically) to not overwhelm the other person.

Now, how should you show up to set the stage for getting the best answers? As a mindset and behavioral habit going into the interview, you might consider taking advantage of the "chameleon effect," a psychological phenomenon in which people tend to like each other more when they're exhibiting similar body language. This effect, of course, changes in a virtual interview, since there's so little display of body language. But you can make interviewees feel comfortable by getting in sync with them, nodding your head, and giving assent when you agree or hear them. Let them know they have your attention by practicing good listening etiquette. See the Appendix for tools to harness empathy and for more on virtual listening skills.

In this vein, do not mute your audio during the interview unless you know your background noise will be a serious distraction. Ask any comedian what performing over Zoom is like, and you'll hear how it's pretty awful to try to ascertain how jokes are landing and to get the feedback necessary to give the show the right energy. Comedians and professional speakers especially rely on audience feedback, which is like fuel for their next joke or thought statement. Interviewing isn't so different: people crave feedback to know they've been heard and approved of. So any outward signs you can show, both visual and auditory, give the interviewee the feedback loop we as humans crave in a social interaction. See Chapter 3, "'Speaking' So Others Will Understand," for more context on why a smiling face and eye contact can help you connect better with the candidate and put them at ease.

Another component of setting up the interviewee for a successful interview involves giving them a chance to provide the right answer by asking the right question. In advance of hiring for any role, it's important to discuss the skills required with a somewhat outside party—either your manager or a peer—and then consider the questions you could ask to learn about someone's ability to use those skills. For me, this part of the interview often comes down to what one might call a *case study*, though I find that term overused.

Every manager should approach this part of the interview in the right way for them, but as for me, I like to take a specific example of part of the role, create a fairly broad-based question, and ask the interviewee how they would approach it. You might call this a case study, but it's far from some of the more formal examples of case studies that are common in industries such as consulting. For example, as a business-to-business (B2B) marketer, I like to ask how someone would design an email campaign for a specific customer subset. Any marketer should be able to answer this question from a flow perspective, such as first creating segments categorizing their potential audience, then messaging for the segments, and then building a series of automated emails to deliver the messages sequentially to the right audience. For email marketers, I would expect a lot more focus on the technical questions, such as the setup and the open rates. From a product marketer, I would expect more focus on the messaging, the customer, and so on. But each interviewee should at least touch on the aspects that aren't a part of their role, because I can't have people who don't look at the broader picture of *why* we send email marketing.

I am also looking for the structure of their response, their clarity of explanation, and their creativity. I like to spell out these needs to be very clear about what I am looking for. And I also highlight that I am not looking for any technical prowess that falls outside of their role. I can ask other questions to understand which technical aspects of, say, pay-per-click (PPC) marketing I would expect them to have.

Using empathy in an interview is also a great opportunity to really look for clues in the candidate's answers that go beyond the ostensible content of the responses. There's a whole subtext to the answer that is really the crux of the question. As you listen to their answers, consider: What do they focus on? By their emphasis, excitement, or tone of voice, where do they put their energy? This comes through no matter where the interview is held, virtually or in real life. You can hear the difference between a rote answer and something someone genuinely is passionate about. For some people, this will be the pace of speaking or modulation of volume. For others, this will be the percentage of time given to any one aspect of the answer or the order in which they structure their response.

Virtual hiring and other trends have increased the prevalence of behavioral questions, mostly starting with "Tell me about a time when . . ." because the answer can be very revealing of how a person approaches work. These more open-ended questions are particularly useful in evaluating how people structure an answer. This structure or focus is even more important when you have fewer visual cues about their state of mind. It's hard not to elaborate on pieces of a story or strategy that aligns with someone's strengths or where they were really able to shine. People will tend to gloss over areas where their skills are weaker or times when they were less involved. Questions that don't have a natural structure, such as behavioral questions with the expected STAR (situation, task, action, result) response or a case study, can be particularly revealing. You can ask questions such as "What energizes you at work?" or "What's an example of something relevant that you've seen?" And I always ask, as a marketer, "What's the best B2B marketing campaign you've seen?" These questions also provide a prime time to show off what they know about the company they are interviewing for, by tying their skills and strengths into the role or organization. I'm always shocked by people who don't do basic research before an interview.

In short, when someone uses an indirect means of communication, such as elaborating on certain aspects of their work, to tell you how they like to spend their time, listen to them! And then figure out whether their response aligns with the role. If so, great! If not, be sure to clear this up, or consider how to change the role if the person is really great. You don't want there to be a mismatch.

Don't be afraid to redirect more than you would in an in-office interview. If you are listening to an answer and they seem to be veering off toward a different train of thought, interject and give them a chance to correct themselves. People are not mind readers and don't necessarily know what you are looking for. It can be much harder virtually to reflect back the direction you are looking for, especially if they can't see your body language. I usually give two nudges in the direction of the type of answer I am looking for. Here are some things you can say:

- "Let's go back to the original focus of the question. What I really want to focus on is X."

- "This is a really comprehensive background. Can you tell me more about your specific actions or goal?"

If they can't follow the correct format with help, then maybe they really aren't the right person. But I want to reiterate: just because an answer didn't come out immediately the way you wanted it to is not an automatic fail. There are two reasons to step back from this snap judgment. First, your intention is to make the person comfortable. You are taking their perspective to understand how they might be stressed by this interview, but their stress is not an indication of their ability to do the job. And second, working with people who do things differently than you is inherently valuable. It's important to create a culture of differing viewpoints. These perspectives lead to better decision-making in the long run.

Another example where you really want to listen to what is being said indirectly is asking why they are leaving their current job. Again, in an in-person interview, this would be a time when physical cues could really help you to read between the lines. It's much harder to tell if someone is taking a defensive, arms-crossed pose or unconsciously avoiding eye contact as they stretch the truth if you're on videoconference. Without these clues, you need to pay close attention. There are tons of good reasons to leave a job, but here are some red flags that come up:

- If you ask why they are leaving their last job, but you hear a lot about what they are looking for in their new role, what are they not saying about what's happening at their old job?

- Look for negative word choices. They can be indicative of a negative perspective or a working environment that is unsupportable for them. These choices indicate a good place to dig deeper. Someone who's categorically unhappy in their role—and I've met quite a few—is not someone you want on your team. Someone who plays the victim often tends to repeat that behavior, saying it's not their fault they couldn't succeed.

- Another subtle indirect communication clue to look out for and question, particularly in management roles or roles with a lot of cross-team collaboration, is the interviewee's balance between ownership of efforts and success—and giving credit to others. I like to listen very carefully to the use of the word *I* versus *we*. It's hard to give a hard-and-fast rule for how much someone should lean in either direction, but if you pay attention and the ratio of *I* versus *we* feels off for the situation, you should ask more questions. You want to understand exactly what someone did in each scenario. For a manager, it's okay and a part of the job not to actually do the hands-on work. For an individual contributor, you need to hear which particular parts they did, if they were involved in a group effort. Do you want someone on your team who takes credit for things they didn't do? Probably not.

Again, interviews are not battlegrounds. I have seen many managers, particularly in the start-up world, interview in a way that seems as if they are trying to trip up the other person, asking questions in a pointedly antagonistic way. Is this the kind of job that requires thinking on your feet in high-stress situations? If that's not a factor in success, it shouldn't be a factor in the interview process. This is a terrible way to create psychological safety.

If the goal of the interview is to find out about the person's knowledge and personality, why would you want them to convey this information under duress?

This is the point where empathetic interviewing comes in. How do you use the concepts discussed earlier in this book—creating rapport and psychological safety, putting yourself in another person's shoes, and thinking about subconscious cues—to help you hire the best person for the role? Interviewing is harder virtually; you don't want to set people up to fail because of your attitude. And in a video or phone call, it's harder to mitigate the aggression of your words and voice with other nonverbal cues; you risk being reduced to that one attribute.

Interviews aren't perfect; any great, tenured manager knows that sometimes you just get it wrong. A study by Barrick, Shaffer, and DeGrassi tracked impression management by candidates and found that candidates who were successful in managing the interviewer's impressions of their superficial attributes, like appearance and speech patterns, did not have better performance later in their ratings after they had the job.[5] Another study looked at whether interviewers could rate people against the criteria of conscientiousness and emotional stability and found that most interviewers could not.[6] And yet, emotional stability and conscientiousness tend to be the most correlated with future on-the-job performance.[7] The authors hypothesized that interviewees were most able to manage those aspects during an interview and present a better version of themselves, but that did not predict their ability to do the required task. More structured interviews tended to reduce these inaccuracies and over-rating for conscientiousness and emotional stability, but not by much. What should these findings tell you? At the end of the day, interviews can only be trusted so much.

You can get better at making people comfortable in interviews by mock interviewing, having someone else sit in to critique you, or if legally allowed, recording interviews to understand where you could do better. With working from home now the norm, it's much easier to do mock interviews and oversee peers practicing and providing feedback, because having someone critique is less noticeable if they are a muted, black square on a videoconference screen.

What Virtual or Technology Format Should I Use?

Use multiple formats for your interviews to test how they work in different situations. And also consider whatever formats and channels the role will require and what your team uses. Technology in this space is constantly evolving, but broadly, you should consider what these formats may teach you about the candidate:

- If the role requires extensive written work, interview at least partially via writing to assess those skills.

- As we've discussed, Zoom can be more draining than the phone, so it may show you a different side of their personality.

- You could even give candidates a few questions in advance to be answered via short one- to two-minute videos. Beyond the content of the response, videos also allow you to evaluate a candidate's conciseness, ability to follow direction, and comfort with the unexpected. You should ask the same question of all candidates so that you can compare videos later. This way, you can get other team members' opinions without adding interviewers to the panel.

How Can I Avoid Bias to Increase Diverse Thinking on My Team?

People often talk about fit in the context of hiring—making sure you get the right fit for the team, culture, and so on. But, of course, what constitutes "fit" for the interviewer could lead to some pretty unhealthy biases. Any time you are wondering about fit, it's good to ask yourself: "Would not fitting in—for example, bringing diversity of thought—be of value in this role?" It's important to foster a cohesive team, but you don't want a team where everyone is too similar—too many extroverts, too many MBAs, too many creatives.

Superficial rapport is the camaraderie that comes from having enough in common with another person to quickly make a judgment about getting along with them. While there are concrete indicators, like being alums from the same school or being from the same town, style of dress or accent can also reveal superficial bonds. It's natural to use heuristics to categorize people; evolutionarily, this was a requirement for quickly sizing people up. However, in the modern workplace, these superficial indicators lead to bias and do little to improve the culture or engagement of a workplace.

The obvious: if you can't see the person, you aren't as affected by visual cues—race, physical disabilities, and so on—and are less likely to be biased in your initial interaction. For this reason, making initial screening calls via phone is my preferred first step, even beyond HR, because it removes bias and makes people more comfortable. Leave the hot seat of a Zoom call for when the candidate pool has been narrowed down. Also, as we all know, Zoom calls are draining for all participants, and screening multiple candidates over Zoom in the early stages of a hiring process may not be a good use of your own energy. If people in Jane Austen's time could build entire love affairs using pen, paper, and a rudimentary postal system, surely we can use our modern technology to make hiring decisions without seeing people in person.

What Is My Gut Saying?

Yes, you can trust your gut, too. While using tools to prevent bias—such as asking the same questions, using a hiring panel, and typing up notes immediately after an interview—goes a long way toward fighting bias, it's not unreasonable to use your gut in making decisions about hiring. Studies have shown that humans can rapidly deduce specific information about others, such as their intelligence.[6] People's ability to accurately assess such traits varies, so it's a useful exercise to think back and even make careful notes comparing *what you thought about someone in an interview* versus *how they eventually performed.* Comparing can help you uncover biases and highlight times where your gut was right. This exercise might also remind you not to discount the signals you sense.

Even over video, we can make valuable judgments quickly. Studies of teachers show that even using very short video clips, people's snap judgments of the teachers' capabilities were closely aligned with the end-of-year reviews by students, even accounting for their attractiveness, which can affect this type of rating.[7]

Interviews are inherently time-bound, which demands a level of efficiency. Having a more structured process—with candidates answering all of the same questions, including a formulaic case study—allows you to measure candidates quickly on the metrics that matter to you, including the softer skills.

What If They Have a Major Technical Snafu?

Realistically, technical incidents will bias you. Should they? Some people are ill prepared and don't have a professional setup for videoconferencing to reflect accurately how they would approach the job. Let's assume their setup isn't reflective of their ability; in that case, you need to find some mitigating strategies to offset these imbalances in technology. To start with, use the minimum amount of technology to acquire what you need to know. Forget trying to win friends and influence people over Zoom; start with over the phone! A phone call can be a lot easier to focus on when you're truly trying to convey information. Or can you start with video and then turn it off? One nice approach might be to start with video to develop a bit of rapport and understand something about their physicality and how they present themselves, but then move to audio only when you're discussing their background.

If you really want to focus on what they are saying, it's easier if you can only hear them. This approach obviously takes away the chance to read someone's body language. But with poor internet connections and the awkwardness of the screen size, how much is that extra visual information worth? Our voices also can give away a lot. Humans are able to discern each other's emotions from different aspects of speech, like sadness or anger, just from the pitch of someone's voice.[8]

One factor I must flag, but I think the jury is still out on the best practice in this area, is how to conduct panel interviews over videoconference. Interviewing this way goes against everything we know about how humans can take in information virtually. It's exhausting and basically impossible to read the reactions of four different people as little squares in Zoom. This interaction is markedly different from an in-office experience, where body language is much more pronounced. There, watching facial cues is easier, and there isn't the need for total silence because of the overlap of interrupting people. My current suggestion is that the candidate should present a case study to a group, just as one would present ideas naturally in meetings. But then questions should come in subsequent one-on-ones, where each participant has to focus on only one or possibly two people at a time. This way, everyone has some anchor to justify their evaluation of the content and effectiveness of the presentation, but the candidate doesn't have to fight the uphill battle of creating intimacy with four little squares on the screen. Still, it's valuable to have multiple opinions, particularly when you can't meet in person. So it is important that the candidate meets the team.

How Will I Sell the Role?

How do you describe yourself and the team? Your "pitch" requires practice because you want to honestly help people self-select for the situations that fit them, to the extent that they are self-aware enough to select the best environment for their skills and preferences. But you don't want to scare people off. Common questions and situations come up regarding work-life balance, sources of conflict or competing interests within the company, and how the hierarchy or business structure enhances or impedes getting work done. In a virtual interview, candidates are missing a lot of the physical context about the work environment—such as noise level, type of seating, or desk cleanliness—that give them clues about your organization.

In advance of interviewing candidates, it's good to think about how to best describe the firm in the context of a group of humans working together.

How do they communicate, have fun, or deal with conflict? Talk about these descriptions with others on the team to make sure that your perspective on these axes, or other important ones, jibes with the rest of the team. One person's perfect work-life balance might be another's worst nightmare. Some things you might want to cover:

- Hours

- What you've done to promote culture or team bonding

- Benefits that specifically relate to the firm's culture

- Stories of career paths and progressions, both the extraordinary and the more common

- Communication preferences and formats, how meetings are handled, how Slack is utilized, whether you send lots of WhatsApps

As you formulate messages to help candidates understand your organization, getting a couple of examples from diverse people illustrating why it's great to be on this team may help. It's hard to know what positive aspects may resonate with someone, particularly someone you just met an hour ago. You want to paint as full and realistic a picture as you can, within the concise time frame of an interview. As an empathetic interviewer, as best possible, put yourself in their shoes and think what might matter. You will learn about the candidate from their answers, and inadvertently or expressly, they will give you indicators of what kind of work environment they are looking for.

Virtual interviewing has one benefit now that WFH or hybrid appears to be the long-term norm. That is, it is a good indicator of the skills required to communicate at the office. We will all need to know how to bond, present, negotiate, and work online for the foreseeable future. Judging people based on digital-only criteria can feel limiting, but with practice and preparation, it might be just what you need to pick the best remote candidates.

CHAPTER 10

BEING INTERVIEWED REMOTELY

AS THE INTERVIEWEE, YOU can feel as if there's an even greater power imbalance in a virtual interview, where you aren't gathering any information about the company's vibe or culture from what you see in their office, including the people in it. Here's how to make the best of this situation and manipulate the virtual scenario to put your best foot forward:

- Prepare for a structured interview.

- Get your Zoom basics in order.

- Aim for a comfortable conversation.

- Heighten your empathy: use active listening and gauge their reactions.

Prepare for a Structured Interview

I've noticed that remote interviews tend to be more structured than in-person interviews, with a very clear set of behavioral questions, asked without an apparent flow or context, almost as if picked from a list. The reasons could be that managers' calendars have gotten even more packed in work from home, they're making an effort to remove bias, or chitchat might feel a bit awkward virtually. Whatever the reasons, you should be prepared for more structured interviews, without a flow from one question to the next. And regarding your answers, remember it's hard to be an engaging storyteller over Zoom—not impossible but harder than in person—thus, you need to rehearse your stories so that they are clear and concise, and they get your point across.

Virtual delivery is harder than in-person delivery. You can't easily use hand gestures, and the interviewer's gaze is unnaturally directed very closely at your face. Being the interviewee is much like being an evening news anchor, which means you want to emulate their techniques. For your story, think like a journalist. You want to be factual and as brief as possible while covering everything. And be engaging. The first step is to craft and deliver a well-structured answer. Great answers have a beginning, middle, and end: lay out the setting clearly, explain any industry jargon, and directly address the interviewer's question. It's always helpful to close with a recap of the interviewer's question, to remind them both what they asked and how effectively you answered it.

When it comes to concrete efforts to practice your structure, the gold standard is the STAR method (situation, task, action, result). I highly recommend looking up great examples of STAR responses to think about your structure. But I also like to take the structure considerations a bit further. Given that you are already channeling an evening news anchor, borrow a few other tried-and-true public-speaking techniques. Remember the often-repeated rule of three: "Tell 'em what you're going to tell 'em, tell 'em, and tell 'em what you told 'em." This technique functions like a guide for the listener, similar to giving them both a clear table of contents and a final summary so that they know what to walk away with.

You also want to practice your STAR responses for a *star* delivery. Think of your answers like a movie and deliver your answers like a Hollywood star. Obviously, I don't want you to do this in a cheesy or overly dramatic way, but I do want you to be able to channel your inner theater kid. That means conveying with passion your beginning, middle, and end. In Chapter 3, "'Speaking' So Others Will Understand," we covered how pitch and volume modulation affect persuasiveness, and it's useful to weave those improvements into your interviews.

The last thing you can do to make your interview feel more comfortable is to start with something many of us find extremely uncomfortable: you may want to record and check your body language. Recording yourself lets you see where your weird Zoom traits are. For example, if you gesticulate a lot with your hands, you will want to find a way to do that within the confines of your camera angle so that your communication style comes through.

Speaking of newscasters, journalists also do their research, and they prepare what they want to say. As in any interview, researching the company, team, and whatever other information you can find and crafting questions and anticipated answers ahead of time will help you deliver solid and engaging answers.

Get Your Zoom Basics in Order

Zoom etiquette has been repeated a thousand times, but I still see people failing at it. Your voice. Your outfit. Making sure the tech works. These ideas have been hammered home, but I still see people with issues that they could have avoided. Get a friend to do a practice run with you . . . and bonus points if you film it. In short, make sure your sound is good, your face is shown straight on, and there's nothing super weird or distracting in the background you can remove. We covered this information in Chapter 3, "'Speaking' So Others Will Understand," and it's worth reviewing all those superficial opportunities for improvement with every interview.

This advice also applies to creating a space that feels as though it's different, even just a little, to tell your brain that this is a novel and important experience. We covered neuroarchitecture in Chapter 2, "Feeling Good Working from Home," and it's worth reflecting on which aspects of a unique work environment would make you feel more like you were at an interview. Briefly, you might do the following:

- Consider your outfit. Definitely put on shoes.
- Close out things on your screen that might remind you of your current work.
- Clean off your desk.
- Try to schedule the meeting so that you're not "running" into it from another meeting and can take a moment to change your headspace.

- Do a Superman pose. Even spending a few minutes doing something physically centering tells your brain you're doing something new here.

- If there's a tech snafu, be prepared to roll with it. Wi-Fi dies. Children enter unexpectedly. The benefit of everyone having tested out working from home is that the expectations for professionalism have changed. That being said, how you deal with interruptions is a reflection of your character and your preparedness. Demonstrate your accountability and calm-headedness, and have your backup solutions ready: charged cell phone, extra headphones, and so on. Try not to let the unexpected rattle you.

Aim for a Comfortable Conversation

Think about your casual chats, and try to make your interview have a similarly comfortable feel, without being sloppy or too informal. You want the interviewer to know about you, just as much as you need to know about them. If this type of human give-and-take doesn't come up in the beginning, use some of the time allotted at the end to ask more direct questions about your interviewer: how they got to their role, what they like best about the culture and the organization, how it's different from their previous role, and so on. Showing off your personal side is beneficial for you, particularly as studies have shown the quality of the non–job-related chat is correlated with getting the role.[1] It's easier to propose this more casual conversation on the premise of finding out more so you can understand what it's like to work with this person. Also, everyone loves to talk about themselves, so this conversation helps to put the interviewer in a positive mindset.

Silence is awkward at the best of times and feels even more so in virtual interviews. If you need a moment to think, say so. Give the interviewer that context, to let them know you're taking the question seriously and want to give a thoughtful answer. Obviously, this kind of response isn't great if the question is "Tell me about your background," but for more open-ended questions, don't rush.

You can make use of your home environment. As I said, virtual interviews tend to be more transactional, so you should make sure to hit all the points in the questions in an effective and logical manner. This is one way in which WFH is better than in person; you can have your notes in front of you. Take advantage! Tack up sticky notes around your screen providing salient points to your answers to common questions. Write things down as the interviewer says them so you know what to cover in your answers. This tip comes with a caveat, however: you can't use this strategy to cheat. Reading out answers to questions that you don't truly understand will be obvious to the listener, who can see your eyes darting to the side.

Heighten Your Empathy

Once again, as with so many components of a hybrid setting, take advantage of your digital empathy skills to connect with the interviewer as best as possible. To put yourself in a place to read their face and nonverbal signals, tape something over your image or turn it off. While we can't re-create being in person, mirroring their physical behavior and giving active listening clues—such as nodding, murmuring assent, and really just generally appearing interested—are still very important in online conversations. Also, don't mute for this reason unless you have to. No one likes talking into a void!

In the same vein, look for the clues the interviewer is giving you. When you're not in the room with someone, it's harder to tell if your answer is going off-track. Look for clues of discomfort or gentle attempts at interruptions, like coughs and throat clearing, to tell you that you should wrap it up. Or find out if you're answering the question they are looking for by asking something like, "Does that answer your question, or were you looking for something else?" It's okay to sync up with the interviewer. Working with fewer nonverbal clues means you have to lean harder on verbal ones.

When you're in a position to do so, it's good to figure out whether this call needs to be by videoconference. Making this decision as the interviewee can be hard, as there's an implicit power imbalance in looking for a job. But we as humans can process auditory information very effectively, perhaps more effectively than video calls. As we've discussed previously, videoconferences can be tiring, distracting, and stressful. I'd therefore argue it definitely doesn't have to be the norm. So if you want to be able to harness your empathy effectively and understand the interviewer's perspective, using the phone might be a better choice. Then you only have to process their auditory clues, which tend to be clearer and less affected by technology, like erratic Wi-Fi or an awkwardly placed camera.

Most likely, your interviewer will take notes, which may require looking down. This behavior in Zoom can make you feel as though they aren't listening. Be prepared to keep speaking calmly and enthusiastically, even if they look away. Most likely, they can still hear you, but they are jotting something down, either using the keyboard or writing by hand.

Lastly, if you're doing a presentation, remember what it's like to watch presentations yourself. They are only on your screen; you sometimes can't see the participant's face, depending on the technology, and viewers are perhaps even more likely to zone out. Make sure your slides have the right kind of information and are the right size for this environment. Eliminate fonts you have to put your nose to the screen to see. Practice your delivery even more than you would have in person; you can't use body language—even facial expressions, depending on the software—to create a more engaging story. You have only your voice and words.

Most importantly, while this whole setup feels awkward, it is the way of work now. You will be presenting virtually, meeting new people over Zoom, and being reduced to your avatar in a professional setting for the foreseeable future, if not forever. And so will everyone else. This type of interview is reflective of the role and how you'll interact with your colleagues, so while it can require different contingencies, it shouldn't be much more stressful than an old-fashioned, in-person one.

CHAPTER 11

NETWORKING, MENTORING, AND MAKING NEW DIGITAL FRIENDS AT WORK

Getting ahead in the workforce has always required networking and charm, and a move away from in-person events cannot erase this fact. But if you can't run into people at conferences, sidle up to them in the hallway, or sit next to them in the conference room, how do you network with others? How do you connect at work or within your industry to build your professional knowledge, find mentors/mentees, and grow your career?

Who Do You Want to Be Online?

What are you conveying to people? The first part of your message is *you*. Everything you do online and on social media is colored by who you are, how you speak, how you deliver content, and what images you post. When you're trying to hone your empathy skills, it's good to be thoughtful about how you appear to others. We covered more on the superficial in Chapter 3, "'Speaking' So Others Will Understand."

More deeply, there are three traits you want to harness in optimizing your impression management:

- Credibility
- Confidence
- Humility

They are inextricably linked, but let's unpack them one by one for tips on how to embody each more effectively.

CREDIBILITY We start with *credibility*, which has two facets:

- Do I actually know enough to be an expert in this scenario?
- Can I present myself in a way that others believe I am an expert?

You should start by asking yourself, "Do I know enough about a situation to make decisions that others will respect?"

People are watching each other at all times and assessing how trustworthy their peers are. A study from VU University in Amsterdam found that people's trustworthiness diminished if they publicly engaged in behaviors that suggested low willpower, like overeating.[1] This opportunity for observation and judgment has changed a lot in the pandemic; we can hide a lot more now! But that overweights what people can see, if they are getting a smaller slice of your personality. It's essential to consider that all of your actions at the office are telling a story to your colleagues.

A funny thing about credibility is that humans tend to be forward-looking. Although it's a logical way to build credibility, harkening back to your past success may not have the desired effect. A Harvard and Stanford study showed participants who were evaluating two similar job candidates to determine their fit for a leadership position. One had two years of relevant job experience and high scores on a test of leadership achievement. The other had zero years of relevant job experience and high scores on a test of leadership potential. Who got the job? The study participants believed the second candidate—who had no experience but great leadership potential—would be better suited for the role.[2]

One way to establish credibility, if it's of interest to you to do so, is to become active on LinkedIn or Twitter in your industry. This route has worked for many people, though it requires considerable effort. On a very practical note, you can also establish greater credibility with your voice tone by speaking at the low end, but not the bottom, of your vocal range. We looked at the value of a low voice in Chapter 3, "'Speaking' So Others Will Understand," but here we are adding credibility to the list of things a low voice connotes.

We've all seen speakers overcompensate for their tone, pushing their voices too low, into a range that sounds false and put on. Hardly credible. And obviously, a too high-pitched voice can sound uptight or frantic. It's worthwhile to record yourself speaking higher and lower, testing out what feels comfortable, and then get some honest feedback from friends and family on different registers that you can comfortably hold. For parents with small children, this is a great two-for-one; recording your one-hundredth version of *Winnie the Pooh* is great for understanding how you sound. This knowledge is even more useful in a time of video and voice calls. Since we can't give as much context with our bodies, we need to be more thoughtful across the board about things we can control, like our voice.

Though changing your facial expressions might feel like a bridge too far, one study found that what people perceive as a neutral face, with mouth and eyebrows slightly upturned, makes people look more trustworthy.[3] The study also found facial cues conveying trustworthiness are malleable, but facial cues conveying competence and ability are less so. This means that while you can influence how trustworthy others perceive you to be, it's harder to make yourself seem more competent. Particularly in a videoconference setting, where your face takes on more importance due to the lack of additional body language, it's worth practicing to convey the appropriate facial expressions.

Eye contact, though this is significantly more difficult in a Zoom-only world, is also key. Studies have shown that people who make eye contact while speaking are consistently judged as more intelligent.[4] As vain as it sounds, you should try taking some photos or videos of yourself presenting and figuring out what looks the most natural. It's hard to know what eye contact looks like on a video call without some practice, because looking at the camera is not our natural inclination.

CONFIDENCE The second thing you'll want to convey to manage others' impression of you is *confidence*. Consider how you are delivering your thoughts to others, not just the substance of your message. If you speak at a rapid clip, for example, lobbing information at your listeners, they'll feel like your opponents. Rapid speaking also conveys nervousness. Speaking slowly and calmly, conversely, conveys confidence. Adding excessive examples and extraneous proof to sell your idea can also feel invasive and combative to the other person.

The reaction of most people to having anything—ideas, balls, unidentified flying objects—lobbed at them in rapid-fire succession is to *duck* or to *defend*. In a business scenario, defending means starting to collect more evidence of why they didn't trust you in the first place.

You can't build credibility by going on the offensive.

Confidence is particularly useful when you're a young manager. You want your direct reports to believe you know what you're doing. Being able to convey confidence and credibility will go a long way toward gaining the respect of your team, not to mention your other colleagues and those in your network.

There are some actions and tactics that inherently appear confident that you can use to your best advantage:

- Speaking at a measured pace—not too slow, not too fast.

- Speaking on the lower end of your pitch register.

- Sitting or standing with good posture. While you can't see as much of your posture over a video screen, hunched shoulders can be visible. And body language is as much for you, to put you in the right frame of mind, as for those who can see you.

- Initiating the conversation or idea flow. Be the person willing to move the conversation forward or open the room to new ideas.

- Asking questions. Being able to turn the attention from yourself to those around you implies you aren't needy or desperate to get your point across.

That's an interesting knock-on effect from many of the actions you might take to increase or improve your credibility in your professional network. Your direct reports are most certainly watching you, so all of these are management techniques as well, positioning yourself as a valuable expert.

HUMILITY And lastly, as you manage your impression, you will want to embody *humility*. Having humility may seem somewhat contrary to having confidence, but in reality, it is tightly linked, not antithetical. It's okay, great even, to take pride in your work, but you want this to appear as a realistic sense of confidence that shows modesty. This path can be tricky for anyone to take—how to explain your skills and qualifications without bragging. There are three main ways to make self-promotion more humble:

- Be careful of your *I* versus *we*. Giving some credit to others, even when you also explain your integral role, reminds people that you are a team player and understand that nothing gets done in a silo.

- Make sure they have the context of the situation—for example, the size of the team you led, the amount of revenue the deal brought in, or the academic reputation of your alma mater. Don't continue explaining how fantastic these attributes are. Of course, you need to make sure that the listener understands your MBA is from Harvard, but after you're sure they have that context, repeating that your MBA is from Harvard doesn't add useful context and can be seen as bragging.

- Don't be vague or obtuse in an attempt to be coy. Repeatedly referencing going to school in New Haven as part of your credentials is rather smarmy. Going to Yale is a fantastic achievement and certainly a part of your success, but being vague about the fact, to entice the listener to want to know more, is off-putting for those who "get it" and confusing for those who don't.

I think humility is a big part of the Ben Franklin effect, which says if you ask someone for a favor, they are more likely to help you later than if you had not begun by requesting a favor. This effect has been shown in academic studies as well as in Franklin's personal life. In his autobiography, he tells the story of an adversary. He wrote to this adversary and asked to borrow a rare book, in an effort to convert this man into a friend. Franklin noted, "He that has once done you a kindness will be more ready to do you another, than he whom you yourself have obliged." The adversary sent him the book, which was the beginning of a longstanding friendship.[5] To me, this is a story about humility and opening yourself up to the other person, putting yourself on a perceived lower level than them. You are reducing the feeling of competition between the two parties.

You can also even test out The Favor Request, made famous in a study from Georgetown University. A salesperson suggests to the prospective consumer to consider doing a favor. For instance, as the consumer ponders the offer to buy some art, the salesperson adds, "In fact, at this price, I hope that the next time you hear about somebody looking for art, you consider recommending my gallery." The study showed that the favor request significantly increases acceptance of discounted offers. People who were asked for something in the end were more likely to buy the art.[6] As they say, "Help me, help you."

In short, if you manage to convey humility, you'll be less likely to threaten your colleagues' self-esteem, and your mistakes won't elicit nearly as many cheers from your "cubemates."

Platform and Identity Management

Your personal brand is something that exists for people you do and don't know. That is, your online identity says something about you even when you're not in the room.

Your LinkedIn and Twitter profiles, particularly, tend to be considered professional and well within the realm of things potential employers, colleagues, mentors, and mentees check out while looking for information about you. I think there's an argument that Facebook and Instagram tend to be more personal. Thus, having those profiles private and not searchable might be your best bet, but this is industry dependent. At least, you must be aware that people will see your public posts, so don't post anything that you don't want your boss hearing about, even if indirectly. There have also been many privacy changes on social networks and there certainly will continue to be more, so it's worth thinking about anything you post, no matter how secure you think it is from prying eyes. You never know when a setting will change and a private group you were in will suddenly become public.

In an office, you are your own brand. In the digital world, you are your own avatar. No different than doing your hair and wearing a professional outfit, you are putting yourself out there in a physical sense with your online profiles. From that perspective, things like your LinkedIn or Twitter profile photo and blurb should be chosen with care, to convey your intended message. If this is how people will make their first impression of you, don't leave it to chance.

This advice is even more true with video, which captures both your voice and demeanor. If you post videos of yourself publicly, on social media or elsewhere, make sure that they depict you in a favorable light, one that fits with how you want colleagues and managers to see you, both now and in the future. If a video does not represent the "you" that you want to present to the world, don't post it, or have it taken down if you weren't the one to post it.

This assessment of your online self is likely to intensify as more and more of our lives migrate onto the internet. Whenever you publish a tweet, you are conveying yourself. Extraversion and positivity, as well as introversion and negativity, are clear even from a tweet.[7] Assessing how you come across is tied to empathy, being able to perceive yourself as others perceive you. How do you come across from their point of view? Are you someone they'd like to work with?

Sentiment analysis and natural language processing can already translate your language choices into a personality or intelligence assessment. Imagine where that could lead, with recruiters using AI to find candidates purely from their LinkedIn profile, for example. It's crucial to pay attention to what you say and how you say it in the digital public domain.

A specific note about recommendations on LinkedIn: some people and companies take them very seriously, so you should curate them just like any other part of your digital profile. It's incredibly valuable to see notes from former managers detailing your abilities, but it's also very revealing to see recommendations from former direct reports. It's perfectly reasonable to help out your recommenders by telling them which skills and experiences you'd like to highlight in their posts.

What is your goal with professional social media? It's good to have a purpose when deciding how to approach these platforms. Otherwise, they can be an overwhelming source of mindless updates or professional jealousy and anxiety.

Are you trying to use these platforms to start networking discussions? They are a great way to meet people or establish yourself in a conversation. You can do this by joining groups, commenting on other people's published work you find interesting, and showing an educated interest in the topics at hand. If you're actively looking for a job, those techniques might be too subtle; perhaps reaching out to people directly and asking for a coffee chat might be more beneficial. The low barrier to entry with a virtual coffee chat might just convince a stranger you admire to take a chance and have a Zoom call with you.

Virtual Group Events

Industry conferences moved to digital with the pandemic, and it seems in many ways the trend is here for the long run. Regarding hearing an exciting speaker, it's much easier to put on a virtual event, both for the attendees and the speakers, all of whom consider their time precious.

What we lose in a virtual conference, however, is a lot of the networking opportunities. Thankfully, software and event organizers are trying to build a virtual arena where networking feels natural.

While that technology is ever-evolving, there are some overarching ideas to consider when you attend a virtual event:

- Go in with a goal.

- Know the audience.

- Read the room.

GO IN WITH A GOAL Going in with a goal means two things: one is preparation, and the other is outcome. If you are using your valuable time to attend a virtual event, you ought to know what you hope to get out of it, even if serendipity may change that. This means reading up on the speaker if the topic looks as though it will be unknown to you, having your personal blurb ready to introduce yourself if needed, being prepared to get involved on social media—like tweeting about what you're seeing and hearing—and if possible, looking up who else is attending and who you might want to meet.

KNOW THE AUDIENCE Your time is valuable. If you're going to "attend" a virtual event, take advantage of some of the things you can only do virtually, like googling the people in breakout rooms with you. This preparation starts before you even decide to attend. If you are going for networking purposes, you should, as much as possible, be prepared if you find yourself in a breakout room or another more intimate setting with people who will provide value in your network—and to whom you can provide value in turn.

As I said, sometimes serendipity guides what happens at an event, but fortune can always be guided by a little preparation.

READ THE ROOM As always, connecting with others comes down to how they perceive you. At the most basic level, going into an event with a mindset of wanting to learn puts you in an attractive light. On a practical note, you can harness your empathy skills to get more out of an event in three ways:

- When it comes time for an icebreaker, share about yourself first if you're able to. Everyone appreciates someone getting the ball rolling.

- If there's a Q&A, ask questions that get the crowd thinking. The most surefire way to do that is to ask a question that you're gnawing on. Don't ask one just to try to make yourself sound intelligent, and don't ask one that is uselessly controversial.

- Connect people. As we discussed in earlier chapters, people look favorably on those who help them. And helping others to network at a networking event is a value that you can bring to almost any interaction. Consider opportunities to introduce people who have overlapping interests or specialties.

Mentorship

Open your net; the world is your oyster now! With a connection to the internet, anyone anywhere can connect with senior individuals in their field who could provide guidance. Access to top-tier mentors is no longer siloed to metropolitan areas or within specific companies.

Research on LinkedIn or join a Slack group to meet individuals or groups of people to learn from. Use any network you have—university, former company, hometown—to reach out to people and start creating a bond. Getting guidance from experienced leaders is more critical than ever, since on-the-job anecdotal training has decreased without the opportunity to overhear colleagues in the office.

Finding a mentor may require multiple attempts because you need a spark, as in any friendship—a mutual interest and respect. The most natural way to start a virtual mentorship is to approach it organically, from a place of learning. Leaders from all different industries are out there on social media, showing their interests. You can start building an authentic virtual relationship via comments and likes, and then move to a more direct relationship. If people can end up married from commenting on each other's Instagram posts, you can definitely find a mentor by doing the same on LinkedIn. After you've established some rapport, reach out when you have a serious question that they would be uniquely positioned to answer, and ask for a half hour of their time for their advice. Maybe this would-be mentor has time or inclination, or maybe they don't, but this is how it starts.

Once again, you have a chance to show empathy. Keep in mind that while this opportunity to find a mentor is great for those seeking one, it can be overwhelming for people who find themselves in demand for their perspective and guidance. Be receptive to this fact and don't push. Once in a mentor-mentee relationship, see the opportunity from the mentor's perspective and give them a chance to feel appreciated while sharing their knowledge.

A virtual workplace also creates an opportunity to *be* a mentor to a wider net. As the business world focuses on efforts to increase diversity and inclusion, mentorship that's not restricted by geography provides ample opportunity to contribute to the greater good while practicing distilling your learnings and experiences for someone more junior than you.

In summation, virtual connection with people in a work setting can open doors and also close them. Taking advantage of the opportunities and being mindful of the pitfalls will put you in a better place to advance your career, as well as help advance the careers of others. And what better use of empathy in the workplace than paying it forward by helping someone else with less access to these opportunities. The virtual work environment makes it possible to work through previous boundaries and help someone more directly.

Connecting with people, whether they be your direct reports or a stranger you'd like to mentor, requires being able to see them as a human, as someone with their own wants, wishes, and perspectives. Fostering virtual connections is harder and often less fun than its in-person counterpart. While corporate society as a whole manages this shift and begins to create best practices, technological innovations, and opportunities for improvement, everyone who works in this environment still has their day-to-day job to get done.

Conclusion

This book starts by describing how to manage yourself intentionally, because there's no chance of being a good manager to others if you don't have your own house in order. From your mental state to your office setup, being ready to bring your best self to work takes, well, work. And this effort falls far more on the shoulders of employees now, with fewer neuroarchitectural clues coming from your company.

Being a manager to others is a great responsibility, beyond even what you're paid for. I'm sure everyone who reads this book can think of many moments in their career that have been significantly guided by the quality of their manager. You can change the direction of someone's life with good management, and that's also true for bad managers.

Hopefully, designing your management strategy from a place of empathy and taking your team's perspective will build a foundation on which you can both effectively coach your team to their greatest personal heights and drive the most team success. No matter your current abilities for harnessing digital empathy, everyone has room to improve. Connecting with others to get more done together is a vital part of work and critical to personal and professional growth. Good luck!

Appendix

How to Improve Your Abilities to Be Empathetic

Empathy is both an innate human skill and something you can get better at. Following is a list of suggestions I've curated in my research for this book to help you improve on your ability to take other people's perspectives.

1. Follow diverse people on social media, such as Twitter or Instagram, and when they post feelings or opinions you don't understand, make a real effort to see their perspective. You could even ask them to explain more to you in detail about why they feel that way or value that opinion. Obviously, politics and religion are examples that might get a little heated, but hearing about how introverts love to spend their time if you're an extrovert or how yoga has changed the life of a dedicated practitioner if you're a lifelong couch potato can be helpful.

2. Find someone you know who needs help with a skill you are very competent in and work to explain to them how to use that skill, such as baking a perfectly risen souffle or making a financial model in Excel. By telling your best friend or your spouse how you do something you do easily, you can see how their mind approaches something differently.

3. Think through the daily life of people who are very different from you, or go one step further and test it out! What would a religious service be like in a faith that you are unfamiliar with, or a walk through a neighborhood in a very culturally different area from yours? Or a trip to another country? All of these exercises create exposure to different ways of thinking.

4. Check out the Reddit forum called "Change My View," for people look-ing at issues from different perspectives. It's a real eye-opening read.

5. Cultivate curiosity about strangers. George Orwell is an inspiring model. Orwell spent several years as a colonial police officer in Brit-ish Burma during the 1920s. Subsequently, he returned to England determined to discover what life was like for those living at the bottom of society. "I wanted to submerge myself, to get right down among the oppressed," he wrote.[1] He dressed himself as a tramp and lived on the streets of East London with the other tramps, beggars, and vagabonds. The result was his book *Down and Out in Paris and London*, describing the radical change in his beliefs, priorities, and relationships from this experience.[2]

6. Read fiction. Reading literary fiction can help improve your ability to understand other people's mental states, as opposed to pop fiction or nonfiction.[3] Fiction is a great way to embed yourself in another person's perspective, and it's definitely easier to achieve than Orwell's experiment.

7. Join a theatrical group. Studies of kids and teenagers who joined per-forming arts programs showed increases in their measurable empa-thy for those who participated in the theater program, but those who joined visual arts programs did not exhibit the same increases.[4] This phenomenon makes sense if you look at the playbook of great actors who are known to work through the three stages of sensing, process-ing, and responding.

8. Meditate. Some research has shown that compassion can be trained through loving-kindness meditation.[5] Compassion is related to empathy, though not the same. This practice is simple: just sit for a few minutes every day to quietly and systematically send loving and compassionate thoughts to loved ones; someone you are in conflict with; anyone suffering around the world; and yourself through self-compassion, forgiveness, and self-love.

Notes

Chapter 1

1. Oxford Languages, languages.oup.com/.
2. Oxford Languages, languages.oup.com/.
3. Kim Scott, *Radical Candor: Be a Kick-Ass Boss without Losing Your Humanity* (New York: St. Martin's Press, 2019).
4. Center for Creative Leadership (CCL), "The Importance of Empathy in the Workplace," November 28, 2020, *ccl.org.*
5. Ernest H. O'Boyle, Ronald H. Humphrey, Jeffrey M. Pollack, Thomas H. Hawver, and Paul A. Story, "The Relation between Emotional Intelligence and Job Performance: A Meta-Analysis," *Journal of Organizational Behavior* 32, no. 5 (2010): 788–818.
6. Tassilo Momm, Gerhard Blickle, Yongmei Liu, Andreas Wihler, Mareike Kholin, and Jochen I. Menges, "It Pays to Have an Eye for Emotions: Emotion Recognition Ability Indirectly Predicts Annual Income," *Journal of Organizational Behavior* 36, no. 1 (2014): 147–63.
7. Google, "Re:Work," *rework.withgoogle.com.*
8. Matt Robinson and Benjamin Bain, "Whistle Blowing Soars to Record with Americans Working from Home," *Bloomberg*, January 12, 2021, *bloomberg.com.*
9. Ravi S. Gajendran and David A. Harrison, "The Good, the Bad, and the Unknown about Telecommuting: Meta-Analysis of Psychological Mediators and Individual Consequences," *Journal of Applied Psychology* 92, no. 6 (2007): 1524–41.

10. Yalda T. Uhls, Minas Michikyan, Jordan Morris, Debra Garcia, Gary W. Small, Eleni Zgourou, and Patricia M. Greenfield, "Five Days at Outdoor Education Camp Without Screens Improves Preteen Skills with Nonverbal Emotion Cues," *Computers in Human Behavior* 39 (2014): 387–92.

11. Judith Held, Andreea Vîslă, Richard E. Zinbarg, Christine Wolfer, and Christoph Flückiger, "How Do Worry and Clinical Status Impact Working Memory Performance? An Experimental Investigation," *BMC Psychiatry* 20, no. 1 (2020).

12. Gary Christopher and John MacDonald, "The Impact of Clinical Depression on Working Memory," *Cognitive Neuropsychiatry* 10, no. 5 (2005): 379–99.

13. Jeremy A. Yip and Maurice E. Schweitzer, "Losing Your Temper and Your Perspective: Anger Reduces Perspective-Taking," *Organizational Behavior and Human Decision Processes* 150 (2019): 28–45.

14. Elaine Hatfield, John T. Cacioppo, and Richard L. Rapson, *Emotional Contagion* (Cambridge, England: Cambridge University Press, 1993).

15. Stanley Schachter and Jerome Singer, "Cognitive, Social, and Physiological Determinants of Emotional State," *Psychological Review* 70, no. 1 (1963): 121–22.

16. Sigal G. Barsade, "The Ripple Effect: Emotional Contagion and Its Influence on Group Behavior," *Administrative Science Quarterly* 47, no. 4 (2002): 644–75.

17. Adam D. Kramer, Jamie E. Guillory, and Jeffrey T. Hancock, "Experimental Evidence of Massive-Scale Emotional Contagion Through Social Networks," *Proceedings of the National Academy of Sciences* 111, no. 24 (2014): 8788–90.

18. Arik Cheshin, Anat Rafaeli, and Nathan Bos, "Anger and Happiness in Virtual Teams: Emotional Influences of Text and Behavior on Others' Affect in the Absence of Non-Verbal Cues," *Organizational Behavior and Human Decision Processes* 116, no. 1 (2011): 2–16.

19. Peter Totterdell, "Catching Moods and Hitting Runs: Mood Linkage and Subjective Performance in Professional Sport Teams," *Journal of Applied Psychology* 85, no. 6 (2000): 848–59.

20. Michael Argyle and Mark Cook, *Gaze and Mutual Gaze* (Cambridge: Cambridge University Press, 1976).

21. David Mechanic and Sharon Meyer, "Concepts of Trust among Patients with Serious Illness," *Social Science & Medicine* 51, no. 5 (2000): 657–68.

22. Christopher C. Gearhart and Graham D. Bodie, "Active-Empathic Listening as a General Social Skill: Evidence from Bivariate and Canonical Correlations," *Communication Reports* 24, no. 2 (2011): 86–98.

23. Tanya Drollinger and Lucette B. Comer, "Salesperson's Listening Ability as an Antecedent to Relationship Selling," *Journal of Business & Industrial Marketing* 28, no. 1 (2013): 50–59.

24. Eileen Wood, Lucia Zivcakova, Petrice Gentile, Karin Archer, Domenica De Pasquale, and Amanda Nosko, "Examining the Impact of Off-Task Multi-Tasking with Technology on Real-Time Classroom Learning," *Computers & Education* 58, no. 1 (2012): 365–74.

25. Jack Zenger and Joseph Folkman, "What Great Listeners Actually Do," *Harvard Business Review*, November 27, 2019.

Chapter 2

1. Komalanathan Vimalanathan and Thangavelu Ramesh Babu, "The Effect of Indoor Office Environment on the Work Performance, Health and Well-Being of Office Workers," *Journal of Environmental Health Science and Engineering* 12, no. 1 (2014).

2. Byoung-Suk Kweon, Roger S. Ulrich, Verrick D. Walker, and Louis G. Tassinary, "Anger and Stress," *Environment and Behavior* 40, no. 3 (2007): 355–81.

3. Andrea Dravigne, Tina Marie Waliczek, R. D. Lineberger, and J. M. Zajicek, "The Effect of Live Plants and Window Views of Green Spaces on Employee Perceptions of Job Satisfaction," *HortScience* 43, no. 1 (2008): 183–87.

4. Nicholas Bloom, James Liang, John Roberts, and Zhichun Jenny Ying, "Does Working from Home Work? Evidence from a Chinese Experiment," *Quarterly Journal of Economics* 130, no. 1 (2014): 165–218.

5. Lingfeng Bao, Tao Li, Kaiyu Zhu, Xiaohu Yang, Xin Xia, and Hui Li, "How Does Working from Home Affect Developer Productivity? A Case Study of Baidu During COVID-19 Pandemic," *ARXIV.com*, 2021.

6. Microsoft, "Research Proves Your Brain Needs Breaks," April 20, 2021, *microsoft.com*.

7. Geraldine Fauville, Mufan Luo, Anna C. Queiroz, Jeremy N. Bailenson, and Jeff Hancock, "Nonverbal Mechanisms Predict Zoom Fatigue and Explain Why Women Experience Higher Levels than Men," *SSRN Electronic Journal*, April 14, 2021.

8. Jeff Green, "3 Hours Longer, The Pandemic Has Obliterated Work-Life Balance," *Bloomberg*, April 23, 2020, *bloomberg.com*.

9. Qualtrics, "Confronting Mental Health Crisis Stemming from the COVID-19 Pandemic," *qualtrics.com*.

10. Blind, "Enjoying Quarantini's? So Are 32% of Professionals," *Medium*, May 19, 2020, *medium.com*.

11. Juliana Schroeder, Michael Kardas, and Nicholas Epley, "The Humanizing Voice: Speech Reveals, and Text Conceals, a More Thoughtful Mind in the Midst of Disagreement," *Psychological Science* 28, no. 12 (2017): 1745–62.

12. Maria Tomprou, Young Ji Kim, Prerna Chikersal, Anita Williams Woolley, and Laura A. Dabbish, "Speaking Out of Turn: How Video Conferencing Reduces Vocal Synchrony and Collective Intelligence," *PLOS One* 16, no. 3 (2021).

13. Katrin Schoenenberg, Alexander Raake, and Judith Koeppe, "Why Are You So Slow? Misattribution of Transmission Delay to Attributes of the Conversation Partner at the Far-End," *International Journal of Human-Computer Studies* 72, no. 5 (2014): 477–87.

Chapter 3

1. E. L. Thorndike, "A Constant Error in Psychological Ratings," *Journal of Applied Psychology* 4, no. 1 (1920): 25–29.

2. DongWon Oh, Eldar Shafir, and Alexander Todorov, "Economic Status Cues from Clothes Affect Perceived Competence from Faces," *Nature Human Behaviour* 4, no. 3 (2019): 287–93.

3. Eric Hehman, Jessica K. Flake, and Jonathan B. Freeman, "Static and Dynamic Facial Cues Differentially Affect the Consistency of Social Evaluations," *Personality and Social Psychology Bulletin* 41, no. 8 (2015): 1123–34.

4. Nora A. Murphy, Judith A. Hall, and C. Randall Colvin, "Accurate Intelligence Assessments in Social Interactions: Mediators and Gender Effects," *Journal of Personality* 71, no. 3 (2003): 465–93.

5. Sean N. Talamas, Kenneth I. Mavor, John Axelsson, Tina Sundelin, and David I. Perrett, "Eyelid-Openness and Mouth Curvature Influence Perceived Intelligence beyond Attractiveness," *Journal of Experimental Psychology: General* 145, no. 5 (2016): 603–20.

6. Juliana Schroeder, Michael Kardas, and Nicholas Epley, "The Humanizing Voice: Speech Reveals, and Text Conceals, a More Thoughtful Mind in the Midst of Disagreement," *Psychological Science* 28, no. 12 (2017): 1745–62.

7. William Apple, Lynn A. Streeter, and Robert M. Krauss, "Effects of Pitch and Speech Rate on Personal Attributions," *Journal of Personality and Social Psychology* 37, no. 5 (1979): 715–27.

8. William J. Mayew, Christopher A. Parsons, and Mohan Venkatachalam, "Voice Pitch and the Labor Market Success of Male Chief Executive Officers," *Evolution and Human Behavior* 34, no. 4 (2013): 243–48.

9. Joey T. Cheng, Jessica L. Tracy, Simon Ho, and Joseph Henrich, "Listen, Follow Me: Dynamic Vocal Signals of Dominance Predict Emergent Social Rank in Humans," *Journal of Experimental Psychology: General* 145, no. 5 (2016): 536–47.

10. Rindy C. Anderson, Casey A. Klofstad, William J. Mayew, and Mohan Venkatachalam, "Vocal Fry May Undermine the Success of Young Women in the Labor Market," *PLOS One* 9, no. 5 (2014).

11. Norman Miller, Geoffrey Maruyama, Rex J. Beaber, and Keith Valone, "Speed of Speech and Persuasion," *Journal of Personality and Social Psychology* 34, no. 4 (1976): 615–24.

12. Kim Scott, "Chapter 1. Build Radically Candid Relationships." Essay. In *Radical Candor: Be a Kick-Ass Boss Without Losing Your Humanity* (New York: St. Martin's Press, 2019), 3–18.

13. Regina Hechanova, Terry A. Beehr, and Neil D. Christiansen, "Antecedents and Consequences of Employees' Adjustment to Overseas Assignment: A Meta-Analytic Review," *Applied Psychology*, March 10, 2003.

Chapter 4

1. Annamarie Mann, "Why We Need Best Friends at Work," *Gallup*, January 15, 2018, *gallup.com*.
2. Richard L. Daft and Dorothy Marcic, "Chapter 10. Leading Teams." Essay. In *Understanding Management* (Fort Worth, TX: Dryden Press, 1998).
3. David Rock, "Managing with the Brain in Mind: Neuroscience Research Is Revealing the Social Nature of the High-Performance Workplace," *Strategy + Business* 56 (2009).
4. Richard E. Nisbett, Henry Zukier, and Ronald E. Lemley, "The Dilution Effect: Nondiagnostic Information Weakens the Implications of Diagnostic Information" *Cognitive Psychology* 13, no. 2 (1981): 248–77; Markus Kemmelmeier, "Separating the Wheat from the Chaff: Does Discriminating between Diagnostic and Nondiagnostic Information Eliminate the Dilution Effect?," *Journal of Behavioral Decision Making* 17, no. 3 (2004): 231–43.
5. Paul Bloom, *Against Empathy: The Case for Rational Compassion* (New York, NY: HarperCollins, 2018).

Chapter 5

1. James W. Smither, Manuel London , and Richard R. Reilly, "Does Performance Improve Following Multisource Feedback? A Theoretical Model, Meta-Analysis, and Review of Empirical Findings," *Personnel Psychology* 58 (2005): 33–66, *leeds-faculty.colorado.edu*.
2. Richard Boyatzis, " Neuroscience and Leadership: The Promise of Insights," *Ivey Business Journal*, January 2011, *researchgate.net*.

3. Paul Green, Francesca Gino, and Bradley R. Staats, "Shopping for Confirmation: How Disconfirming Feedback Shapes Social Networks," *SSRN Electronic Journal*, September 20, 2017.

4. Paul Caldarella, Ross A. Larsen, Leslie Williams, Howard P. Wills, and Joseph H. Wehby, "Teacher Praise-to-Reprimand Ratios: Behavioral Response of Students at Risk for EBD Compared with Typically Developing Peers," *Education and Treatment of Children* 42, no. 4 (2019): 447–68.

5. Michael Schaerer, Mary Kern, Gail Berger, Victoria Medvec, and Roderick I. Swaab, "The Illusion of Transparency in Performance Appraisals: When and Why Accuracy Motivation Explains Unintentional Feedback Inflation," *Organizational Behavior and Human Decision Processes* 144 (2018): 171–86.

6. Schaerer et al., "The Illusion of Transparency in Performance Appraisals," 171–86.

7. Marie T. Dasborough, "Cognitive Asymmetry in Employee Emotional Reactions to Leadership Behaviors," *Leadership Quarterly* 17, no. 2 (2006): 163–78.

8. Jim Harter and Amy Adkins, "Employees Want a Lot More from Their Managers." *Gallup*, April 8, 2015, gallup.com.

9. Keise Izuma, Daisuke N. Saito, and Norihiro Sadato, "Processing of Social and Monetary Rewards in the Human Striatum," *Neuron* 58, no. 2 (2008): 284–94.

10. Glassdoor Team, "Employers to Retain Half of Their Employees If Bosses Showed More Appreciation; Glassdoor Survey," November 13, 2013, glassdoor.com.

11. Sho K. Sugawara, Satoshi Tanaka, Shuntaro Okazaki, Katsumi Watanabe, and Norihiro Sadato, "Social Rewards Enhance Offline Improvements in Motor Skill," *PLOS One* 7, no. 11 (2012).

12. Shawn Achor, "The Email That Could Help You Live Longer," May 21, 2014, oprah.com.

Chapter 6

1. Erica Volini, David Mallon, and Jeff Schwartz, "Knowledge Management: Creating Context for a Connected World," *Deloitte Insights*, May 15, 2020, www2.deloitte.com.
2. John S. Edwards, "Business Processes and Knowledge Management," *Knowledge Management* (2008): 2538–45.
3. Jason Sandvik, Richard Saouma, Nathan Seegert, and Christopher Stanton, "Workplace Knowledge Flows," National Bureau of Economic Research, January 2020.
4. C. Kirabo Jackson and Henry S. Schneider, "Checklists and Worker Behavior: A Field Experiment," *American Economic Journal: Applied Economics* 7, no. 4 (2015): 136–68.
5. Julia Stoll, "U.S. Video Consumption by Device 2023," *Statista*, July 14, 2021, statista.com.
6. Jacques Launay, Roger T. Dean, and Freya Bailes, "Synchronising Movements with the Sounds of a Virtual Partner Enhances Partner Likeability," *Cognitive Processing* 15, no. 4 (2014): 491–501.
7. Madhura Bedarkar and Deepika Pandita, "A Study on the Drivers of Employee Engagement Impacting Employee Performance," *Procedia—Social and Behavioral Sciences* 133 (2014): 106–15.
8. Ethan S. Bernstein, "The Transparency Paradox," *Administrative Science Quarterly* 57, no. 2 (2012): 181–216.
9. C. Kirabo Jackson and Henry S. Schneider, "Checklists and Worker Behavior: A Field Experiment," *American Economic Journal: Applied Economics* 7, no. 4 (2015): 136–68.

Chapter 7

1. Susan Lund, Anu Madgavkar, James Manyika, Sven Smit, Kweilin Ellingrud, and Olivia Robinson, "The Future of Work after COVID-19," McKinsey & Company, February 18, 2021, mckinsey.com.
2. Matt Martin, "The State of Meetings in 2020: Clockwise," Get Clockwise, February 10, 2020, getclockwise.com.

3. Henrik Bresman, "Changing Routines: A Process Model of Vicarious Group Learning in Pharmaceutical R&D," *Academy of Management Journal* 56, no. 1 (2013): 35–61.

4. Antony Jay, "How to Run a Meeting," *Harvard Business Review*, March 1976.

5. Steven Rogelberg, Cliff Scott, and John Kello, "The Science and Fiction of Meetings," *MIT Sloan Management Review* 48 (2007).

6. Simone Kauffeld and Nale Lehmann-Willenbrock, "Meetings Matter," *Small Group Research* 43, no. 2 (2011): 130–58.

7. Desmond J. Leach, Steven G. Rogelberg, Peter B. Warr, and Jennifer L. Burnfield, "Perceived Meeting Effectiveness: The Role of Design Characteristics," *Journal of Business and Psychology* 24, no. 1 (2009): 65–76.

8. Glenn E. Littlepage and Julie R. Poole, "Time Allocation in Decision Making Groups," *Journal of Social Behavior & Personality* 8, no. 4 (1993): 663–72.

9. Joseph A. Allen, Nale Lehmann-Willenbrock, and Steven G. Rogelberg, "Let's Get This Meeting Started: Meeting Lateness and Actual Meeting Outcomes," *Journal of Organizational Behavior* 39, no. 8 (2018): 1008–21.

Chapter 8

1. Jack Welch, "Chapter 8. Parting Ways." In *Winning: The Ultimate Business How-to Book* (New York, NY: HarperCollins, 2005), 119–30.

2. Kim Scott, "Chapter 2. Get, Give, and Encourage Guidance." Essay. In *Radical Candor: Be a Kick-Ass Boss Without Losing Your Humanity* (New York: St. Martin's Press, 2019), 19–42.

3. Gavin J. Kilduff, Hillary Anger Elfenbein, and Barry M. Staw, "The Psychology of Rivalry: A Relationally Dependent Analysis of Competition," *Academy of Management Journal* 53, no. 5 (2010): 943–69.

4. W. E. Scott and David J. Cherrington, "Effects of Competitive, Cooperative, and Individualistic Reinforcement Contingencies," *Journal of Personality and Social Psychology* 30, no. 6 (1974): 748–58.

5. Sally S. Dickerson and Margaret E. Kemeny, "Acute Stressors and Cortisol Responses: A Theoretical Integration and Synthesis of Laboratory Research," *Psychological Bulletin* 130, no. 3 (2004): 355–91.

6. Steven F. Maier and Linda R. Watkins, "Role of the Medial Prefrontal Cortex in Coping and Resilience," *Brain Research* 1355 (2010): 52–60.

Chapter 9

1. Brian W. Swider, Murray R. Barrick, and T. Brad Harris, "Initial Impressions: What They Are, What They Are Not, and How They Influence Structured Interview Outcomes," *Journal of Applied Psychology* 101, no. 5 (2016): 625–38.

2. Amanda R. Feiler and Deborah M. Powell, "Behavioral Expression of Job Interview Anxiety," *Journal of Business and Psychology* 31, no. 1 (2015): 155–71.

3. Neil R. Anderson, "Eight Decades of Employment Interview Research: A Retrospective Meta-Review and Prospective Commentary," *European Work and Organizational Psychologist* 2 (1992): 1–32.

4. Beth A. Pontari, "Appearing Socially Competent: The Effects of a Friend's Presence on the Socially Anxious," *Personality and Social Psychology Bulletin* 35, no. 3 (2008): 283–94.

5. Murray R. Barrick, Jonathan A. Shaffer, and Sandra W. DeGrassi, "What You See May Not Be What You Get: Relationships Among Self-Presentation Tactics and Ratings of Interview and Job Performance," *Journal of Applied Psychology* 94, no. 6 (2009): 1394–1411.

6. Murray R. Barrick, Gregory K. Patton, and Shanna N. Haugland, "Accuracy of Interviewer Judgments of Job Applicant Personality Traits," *Personnel Psychology* 53, no. 4 (2000): 925–51.

7. Murray R. Barrick and Michael K. Mount, "The Big Five Personality Dimensions and Job Performance: A Meta-Analysis," *Personnel Psychology* 44, no. 1 (1991): 1–26.

8. Nora A. Murphy, Judith A. Hall, and C. Randall Colvin, "Accurate Intelligence Assessments in Social Interactions: Mediators and Gender Effects," *Journal of Personality* 71, no. 3 (2003): 465–93.

9. Nalini Ambady and Robert Rosenthal, "Half a Minute: Predicting Teacher Evaluations from Thin Slices of Nonverbal Behavior and Physical Attractiveness," *Journal of Personality and Social Psychology* 64, no. 3 (1993): 431–41.

10. Carl E. Williams and Kenneth N. Stevens, "Emotions and Speech: Some Acoustical Correlates," *Journal of the Acoustical Society of America* 52, no. 4B (1972): 1238–50.

Chapter 10

1. Brian W. Swider, Murray R. Barrick, and T. Brad Harris, "Initial Impressions: What They Are, What They Are Not, and How They Influence Structured Interview Outcomes," *Journal of Applied Psychology* 101, no. 5 (2016): 625–38.

Chapter 11

1. Francesca Righetti and Catrin Finkenauer, "If You Are Able to Control Yourself, I Will Trust You: The Role of Perceived Self-Control in Interpersonal Trust," *Journal of Personality and Social Psychology* 100, no. 5 (2011): 874–86.

2. Zakary L. Tormala, Jayson S. Jia, and Michael I. Norton, "The Preference for Potential," *Journal of Personality and Social Psychology* 103, no. 4 (2012): 567–83.

3. Eric Hehman, Jessica K. Flake, and Jonathan B. Freeman, "Static and Dynamic Facial Cues Differentially Affect the Consistency of Social Evaluations," *Personality and Social Psychology Bulletin* 41, no. 8 (2015): 1123–34.

4. Nora A. Murphy, "Appearing Smart: The Impression Management of Intelligence, Person Perception Accuracy, and Behavior in Social Interaction," *Personality and Social Psychology Bulletin* 33, no. 3 (2007): 325–39.

5. Benjamin Franklin, "Chapter 10." Essay. In *The Autobiography of Benjamin Franklin* (New York: Pocket Books, 1954), 140–51.

6. Simon J. Blanchard, Kurt A. Carlson, and Jamie Hyodo, "The Favor Request Effect: Requesting a Favor from Consumers to Seal the Deal," *SSRN Electronic Journal*, December 25, 2015.

7. Vivek Kulkarni, Margaret L. Kern, David Stillwell, Michal Kosinski, Sandra Matz, Lyle Ungar, Steven Skiena, and H. Andrew Schwartz, "Latent Human Traits in the Language of Social Media: An Open-Vocabulary Approach," *PLOS One* 13, no. 11 (2018).

Appendix

1. George Orwell, "Chapter 9." Story. In *The Road to Wigan Pier* (London: Collins Classics, 2021), 112.

2. George Orwell, *Down and Out in Paris and London* (Oxford: Oxford University Press, 2021).

3. David Comer Kidd and Emanuele Castano, "Reading Literary Fiction Improves Theory of Mind," *Science* 342, no. 6156 (2013): 377–80.

4. Thalia R. Goldstein and Ellen Winner, "Enhancing Empathy and Theory of Mind," *Journal of Cognition and Development* 13, no. 1 (2012): 19–37.

5. Antoine Lutz, Julie Brefczynski-Lewis, Tom Johnstone, and Richard J. Davidson, "Regulation of the Neural Circuitry of Emotion by Compassion Meditation: Effects of Meditative Expertise," *PLOS One* 3, no. 3 (2008).

Index

About the Author

MCKENNA SWEAZEY is a remote- and hybrid-management author and coach, having spent years working in global organizations, managing remote teams around the world. As an accomplished global executive, both in corporations and start-ups, Ms. Sweazey has had more time to hone her interpersonal relationship skills over Skype, Google Hangouts, Slack, good old-fashioned phone lines, and now Zoom than she'd care to remember. She's also an extremely empathetic person, with a natural inclination to focus on what others are saying and thinking, as well as a focus on developing this trait over the course of her career.

Her career has spanned successful start-ups, from Taboola, where she spent five years and which IPO'd in 2021, to the *Financial Times*, where she served as head of global marketing. This experience has given her insight into how different types of companies function and how those nuances affect how people do their best work remotely. Currently, she is a marketing strategy consultant for brands in the US and Europe.

Her writing and coaching are informed by the skills she has developed over years of managing teams ranging in size from three to twenty-five to be as effective from 6,000 miles away as she is in person. Her passion is helping people harness empathy to better connect with their colleagues to drive success. She holds an MBA from INSEAD and currently resides in Silicon Valley.